A Framework for Research on Professional Development Schools

Jeanne Tunks
Jane Neapolitan

UNIVERSITY PRESS OF AMERICA,® INC.
Lanham • Boulder • New York • Toronto • Plymouth, UK

Copyright © 2007 by
University Press of America,® Inc.
4501 Forbes Boulevard
Suite 200
Lanham, Maryland 20706
UPA Acquisitions Department (301) 459-3366

Estover Road
Plymouth PL6 7PY
United Kingdom

Library of Congress Control Number: 2007927993
ISBN-13: 978-0-7618-3822-7 (paperback : alk. paper)
ISBN-10: 0-7618-3822-8 (paperback : alk. paper)

Contents

Acknowledgments

The collaboration for this book grew out of a series of intense conversations about the "disconnects" observed by several colleagues about PDS research and the apparent need for a framework that could help partnerships design studies that would have a real impact on PDS as part of the school reform movement. These conversations originated at the Annual Meeting of the American Educational Research Association (AERA) in San Diego in April, 2004, and continued at the Maryland PDS Conference a month later. In the winter of 2005, the authors "camped out" for a week in Baltimore and crafted the prospectus for this book, taking numerous breaks for walking, cooking, enjoying 65% cacao chocolate bars and red wine, and viewing an occasional video or two. The quest for finding a suitable publisher led us back to AERA in Montreal in 2005, and ended happily at AERA in San Francisco in 2006. Shortly after AERA, University Press of America offered us a contract, and now our vision has become a reality. Our many thanks to Patti Belcher, our Acquisitions Editor, and to the entire editorial, production, and marketing staffs at UPA. Your suggestions, patience, and years of experience have helped us immensely in this endeavor!

Next, our sincerest gratitude to the National Council for Accreditation of Teacher Education (NCATE) for granting us permission to use the *Standards for Professional Development Schools* as the basis for the theoretical framework for this book. Our many thanks to Arthur E. Wise, President; Marsha Levine, Senior Consultant, PDS Standards Development Project; and Jane Liebbrand, Vice President, Communications. Your enthusiasm and support for our project has encouraged us to spread the word in an effort to make a difference for the future of PDS.

To our many friends and colleagues at AERA's Special Interest Group (SIG) on PDS Research, the Holmes Partnership, the Association of Teacher Educators (ATE), the National Association for Professional Development Schools (NAPDS), the Maryland Professional Development School Network, and the newly formed National Consortium of Professional Development Schools (NCPDS), we appreciate your interest in our work and hope you will find this book to be of service to you in your own quests for researching the impacts of PDS.

Finally, our deepest appreciation of our own PDS partners at the Denton Independent School District/University of North Texas PDS and the Owings Mills/Towson University PDS. You have accepted us as friends and colleagues, students and mentors, and friendly critics and researchers. By embracing us as part of your community, we have traveled together on the path of mutual learning and professional growth. Without your trusting and believing in us, we could never have come this far. Thank you.

FOR JLT: Thank you to Mary Harris and Jean Keller who encouraged me to engage in PDS research at the University of North Texas. A deep appreciation to the college of education faculty, school personnel, district personnel, and interns who helped me study the PDS at UNT. My most sincere thanks to my loving husband Thomas Tunks, for his support, understanding, guidance, and long night conversations about conducting educational research.

FOR JEN: I have learned the most about PDS from those who have "been there and done that." These include my mentor and PDS partner, Greg Bryant, and the Principal of Owings Mills Elementary School, Chet Scott. Thank you for teaching me how to handle the many challenges of partnership work. I have also learned a great deal about PDS research and teacher quality from Marsha Levine and Roberta Trachtman. Thank you for your support and friendship and many hours of listening to me as I tell my own story. And finally, to my beloved family—Olinda, Tony, Chris and Ina, Andy and Lauren, and my unwavering Michael—thank you for making a "significant difference" in all that I do.

Introduction

A framework for conducting research on professional development schools (PDS) couples two well formed entities: Standards for Professional Development Schools of the National Council for Accreditation of Teacher Education (NCATE) and research methods delineated by the American Educational Research Association (AERA). The framework provides PDS workers, albeit university, district, school, graduate students, and candidates, with a means of aligning PDS developmental stages with research potential. The framework offers PDS workers a tool for decision-making and action. The assumption guiding the framework is that knowledge of the developmental stage of the PDS program guides research decisions. The structure of the book guides those decisions with description and example.

SUMMARY OF THE CHAPTERS

Chapter One: The Need for A Developmental Approach for PDS Research

In this first chapter the authors present their rationale for the need for a developmental approach for research on PDS. Informed by PDS research over the past 20 years and practical experience with partnerships for the past 10, the authors raise questions about the *quality* and *effectiveness* of PDS research in light of the vision for inquiry and research set forth by The Holmes Group in its trilogy of reports and the national PDS standards set forth by the National Council for Accreditation of Teacher Education (NCATE). The authors propose a framework that will guide and assist researchers and practitioners in their decision making for designing and implementing research that is effective yet appropriate to partnerships' developmental stages.

Chapter Two: The Holmes Group: A Vision for PDS Research

The authors describe in this chapter how the professional development school movement was established and took hold in the United States over the past 20 years. In response to *A Nation at Risk* in 1983 and other criticisms of the status of teaching and learning in the United States, deans from colleges of education created a consortium lead by Judith Lanier, Dean of Education at Michigan State University. The consortium, named The Holmes Group (after the Dean of Harvard University who reformed teacher education at the beginning of the 20th century) took on the task of articulating a vision for the simultaneous renewal of P-12 education and the teaching profession. The first publication of The Holmes Group, titled *Tomorrow's Teachers*, delineated expectations for teacher education that were based on knowledge of human development, proceeded from a multicultural perspective, and were interactive in nature. The second publication, *Tomorrow's Schools,* envisioned a school-university-community partnership in which new teachers were mentored by expert professionals for the ultimate goal of affecting teaching and learning. This "professional development school" would be akin to a teaching hospital that prepared new professionals in a real world context with real world expectations and outcomes. Unlike laboratory schools for teacher preparation, professional development schools would use existing schools and neighboring institutions of higher education to form partnerships with the specific goals of effecting change in teacher preparation, professional development for teachers, and success in learning for children and adults. Relevant to the focus of this book, an *inquiry stance* taken by all the partners would be the mechanism for connecting the partnership's goals. Inquiry would serve as a catalyst for continuous improvement and sustaining the partnership. The third publication of The Holmes Group, *Tomorrow's Schools of Education*, described how higher education must redefine, reorganize, and redeploy itself in order to bring about these desired changes.

Chapter Three: The NCATE PDS Standards: Inquiry as Part of the Interwoven Fabric

The Standards for Professional Development Schools were established by the National Council for Accreditation of Teacher Education (NCATE) in 2001.

In this chapter the authors examine the standards, highlighting and discussing how inquiry and research are interwoven into the fabric of PDS, not as stand alone directives, but as means for integrating the work and development of PDS partnerships. The standards enable the functions of teacher preparation, professional development, inquiry and research, and student achievement by delineating elements for each of the standards. The standards guide development of partnerships in the broad areas of (1) learning community, (2) accountability and quality assurance, (3) collaboration, (4) diversity and equity, and (5) structures, resources, and roles. Developmental guidelines accompany the standards and help partnerships determine their "standing" on each standard as either *Beginning, Developing, At Standard,* or *Leading.* Partnerships use the standards for assessing the developmental stage of their PDS and for guiding next steps in continuous improvement.

Chapter Four: Analyses of PDS Research: Trends and Implications

In an effort to shed more light on the condition of PDS research at present, the authors analyze a sample drawn from EBSCO host of 450 articles published in 1988-2006. The examination groups the publications into four "eras" that depict the development of PDS as a national movement: eras described as beginning, growing, functioning, and focused on accountability. Trends within and across the eras are described regarding types of research methods used and salient themes that emerge. This examination supports the argument for the need for a developmental approach for research on professional development schools.

Chapter Five: A Framework Using AERA Research Methods and NCATE PDS Standards

The AERA publication *Methods of Research*, provides a careful overview of eight different research methods applicable and recommended in education. The eight methods provide the basis for research protocol in PDS programs. In this chapter the authors explore the eight methods, provide a clear explanation as to why and how these apply to PDS research, and then delineate for the reader the different levels of each method as related to the stages of PDS development. In addition, the authors describe the different skills necessary to apply the different methods, leading to a deeper understanding of the relationship between university and school personnel conducting research both institutionally and within individual PDS programs.

Chapters Six—Nine: PDS Research at the Beginning, Developing, At Standard, and Leading Stages

These four chapters provide substance and examples for a framework for conducting research that is both applicable and practical by connecting inquiry/research choices to the NCATE developmental stages of PDS. Research methods recommended by AERA include: ethnographic, case study, action, philosophic, document analysis, survey, quasi-experimental, and experimental. The authors delineate across the eight research methods, which method and at what level within the method the research might focus, for each stage of PDS development.

Sample research questions pertaining to each stage and matching research methods that best address the questions are portrayed through hypothetical scenarios and case descriptions. These chapters create the connection between the NCATE PDS standards and research recommendations from AERA and provide a framework for decision-making among PDS partners interested in conducting inquiry in partnerships.

Chapter Ten: Summary

In this chapter, the authors reflect on key issues raised in the book and highlight several PDS initiatives that help connect and move forward regional and national efforts for creating high quality research for professional development schools.

Chapter One

The Need for a Developmental Approach for PDS Research

Although professional development schools (PDSs) have been in existence for about 20 years, collaborative inquiry or "impact research" has remained the least understood and utilized function of PDS. The Standards for Professional Development Schools developed by the National Council for Accreditation of Teacher Education uphold that inquiry "is the process through which professional and student learning are integrated," a key concept embedded in the standards. Inquiry helps sustain the other PDS functions of teacher preparation, professional development, and student learning. However, because PDS partnerships find themselves at different (and sometimes fluctuating) stages of development, there is need for a deeper understanding of the PDS Standards that integrate inquiry and how to best use them for conducting research that will ultimately *sustain* collaborations and partnerships. In order for partnerships to take a deliberative approach to inquiry, this understanding must also be supported by *examples and guidelines* for developing research studies that are collaborative and practical in implementation yet credible and meaningful in design. The *No Child Left Behind* (NCLB) legislation mandates more carefully crafted research that addresses "what works" in schools. The related federal government research agencies, particularly the Institute for Education Sciences, affiliated with the NCLB law, mandates carefully crafted research that demonstrates effectiveness of programs as related to academic achievement. After four years of study, a national teacher education panel of the American Educational Research Association (AERA) concluded that many of the accepted practices in teacher preparation are not founded on a solid research base . This is partly due to research designs and methodologies that fall short of capturing the complexity of studying teacher education in a rigorous way. Moreover, there are no national databases on teacher education that would lay the groundwork for such comprehensive research.

Although PDS practitioners might agree there are benefits to the PDS model, such as mutual respect and rapport within the learning community and commitment for collaboration resulting in enhanced teacher preparation and continuing professional development, the research output about PDSs has been generally inconclusive. Some reviews of PDS literature have shown that a large portion of what has been documented does not make its way into the mainstream of research dissemination in the form of papers presented at national conferences and articles in refereed journals. This "fugitive literature" is informal in nature and reflective of the situation of most PDSs: practitioners or practitioner/researchers caught up in the dailiness of school and university life with little resources to plan, implement, and disseminate their research in order to affect substantive changes in policy and practice.

Other reviews of PDS research have noted an abundance of qualitative studies that describe contexts and processes. These studies support the momentum for continuing PDS work at the micro level of implementation where there is a richness of experience within the learning community. However, few experimental or quasi-experimental studies about PDS exist. Finally, other reviews have criticized PDS research in general as not meeting standard criteria for being considered "research."

Partnerships in professional development schools, under pressure to account for the effectiveness of their programs regarding teacher preparation, student achievement, and a myriad of other accountability issues mandated by local, state, and national entities, need some means by which to study effectiveness. While the NCATE PDS Standards suggests the use of inquiry to address these accountability issues, prescription for approach to researching the phenomenon remains illusive. In this book, the relationship between the call for inquiry in the NCATE document and the appropriate methodology aligned with the stages of PDS partnership development are presented as a framework. The intention for creating the framework is to empower PDS workers at all levels to conduct appropriate research, therefore providing local, state, and national organizations with accountability required. In addition, well-developed and implemented research, when published, provides the field with in depth knowledge and understanding that informs the field and encourages growth and increased research through duplicated studies.

BACKGROUND

In *Tomorrow's Schools of Education*, a national consortium of Deans of Education known as The Holmes Group, emphasized improvement-oriented inquiry as one of the basic commitments for establishing professional development schools (see Chapter Two for a comprehensive review of the three Holmes reports). Professional development schools integrate the functions of teacher preparation, professional development, inquiry and research, and student achievement in order to bring about whole school improvement and the simultaneous renewal of the teaching profession. According to The Holmes Group, schools of education "should (1) integrate faculty from schools, school districts, and other educational settings into the research and development activities of the school of education; (2) create opportunities for faculty research in a variety of field settings affiliated with the school of education; and (3) create opportunities for faculty research in collaboration with field-based practitioners." PDS research embodies by its complex nature multiple purposes, multiple outcomes, and multiple experiences.

From 1995 to 2001, NCATE conducted a project to develop and field test standards and assessments for professional development schools. Two contextual factors that influenced the approaches taken to the project were (1) the newness of PDS as an innovation, thus making it vulnerable if standards were established prematurely; and (2) the growing commitment in the education community to establishing standards and assessments as the main strategy for establishing accountability. The intention of the standards was to bring rigor to PDSs so "their potential would not be lost" (p. 99). The standards would also provide a framework for guiding the development of partnerships by using an assessment process with feedback for growth. Policymakers at all levels could use the standards to shape incentives and link PDS to the teacher quality agenda. Ultimately, the PDS standards could serve as a framework for conducting and evaluating research connected to learning outcomes.

Following the development of draft standards in 1998, 20 partnerships representing different stages of development and different organizational types were chosen from a pool of 39 applicants to participate in the field test of the draft standards (p. 105). Participation in the project involved commitment to a three-year process of completing a self-assessment, hosting a site visit by a group of national representatives from other PDS partnerships, and conducting an inquiry project. Participation was also testimony to a unique and community-building experience. The most important change resulting from the field test was the creation of Developmental Guidelines for each standard (p. 119), and relevant to the premise of this book, the integration of inquiry and student learning throughout the standards.

Many individual PDSs as well as statewide networks voluntarily use the standards to guide their work. One state in particular, Maryland, has adapted the standards as part of its policy mandate for teacher education reform. A "cross-fertilization" of ideas occurred between Maryland and NCATE, as leaders from the two groups served on each other's advisory boards and

participated in the process (p. 63). The Towson University/Owings Mills Elementary School partnership was chosen as one of the 20 pilot sites for the
NCATE field test project. Through a series of summer leadership academies,
a statewide cadre of 120 PDS "fellows" worked on examining and refining
the standards, developing guidelines for their implementation, devising pilot
experiences similar to those used by NCATE, and formulating an accountability process by which a college or university's PDS could be formally recognized as operating according to standards (p. 64). Lee Teitel of Harvard
University (formerly of the University of Massachusetts at Boston) played a
key role as a consultant to the Maryland project. His graphic framework, a
pyramid focusing the standards on student learning, depicts both the NCATE
and the Maryland vision of PDS work (p. 65). As a result of this intense
process for teacher education reform, PDSs in Maryland grew from 24 in
1997 to 379 in 2004, with 68 percent of them beyond the beginning level of
development (p. 69).

A FRAMEWORK FOR RESEARCH ON
PROFESSIONAL DEVELOPMENT SCHOOLS

A framework for creating PDS research agendas includes the tenets of the
NCATE PDS Standards and accepted research methods recommended by
AERA. The NCATE PDS Standards establishes four stages of development:
Beginning, Developing, At Standard, and Leading. Criteria for each stage, in
the form of rubrics, guide PDS constituents to determine the developmental
function of a working PDS program. The research methods recommended by
AERA include: philosophical, case study, historical, survey, ethnographic,
artistic, quasi-experimental, and experimental . The framework for developing a PDS research agenda includes three steps: (1) defining the PDS's stage
of development, (2) considering research capacity for the constituents, and
(3) aligning appropriate research method(s) to the developmental stage.

   The framework for research, as described herein, grew from years of doing, reading, and hearing about PDS research at national and regional conferences. While many stories of success and struggle provided good information
on the status of PDS in the field, an organized framework for conducting research remained elusive. The developmental approach couples the aspects of
the NCATE PDS Standards with the protocols and expectations of AERA
recommended research methods. A description of how the framework was
developed is provided in detail in Chapter Five.

REFERENCES

Abdal-Haqq, I. *Professional Development Schools: Weighing the Evidence.* Thousand Oaks, CA: Corwin Press, 1998.
Berry, B., and K. Boles. "Inquiry and Professional Development Schools." In *Professional Development Schools: Confronting Realities*, edited by N. Lauter. New York: The National Center for Restructuring Education, Schools, and Teaching, 1998.
Breault, R. A. "Still Lazy after All These Years: Qualitative Data in Pds Research." Paper presented at the Annual Meeting of the American Educational Research Association, Montreal, Canada, April 2005.
Breault, R., and D. Breault. "Tales, Illusions, and Some Valid Conclusions: What We Might Know About Pdss." Paper presented at the Annual Meeting of the American Educational Research Association, San Diego, CA, April 2004.
Breault, R. A. "Still Lazy after All These Years: Qualitative Data in Pds Research." Paper presented at the Annual Meeting of the American Educational Research Association, Montreal, Canada, April 2005.
Cochran-Smith, M., and K. M. Zeichner, eds. *Studying Teacher Education: The Report of the Aera Panel on Research and Teacher Education.* Washington, DC: American Educational Research Association, 2005.
Holmes Group. *Tomorrow's Schools of Education: A Report of the Holmes Group.* East Lansing, MI: Author, 1995.
Jaeger, R., ed. *Contemporary Methods for Research in Education.* Washington, DC: American Education Research Association, 1988.
Levine, M, and R. Trachtman, eds. *Implementing Pds Standards: Stories from the Field.* Washington, DC
National Council for Accreditation of Teacher Education, 2005.
National Council for Accreditation of Teacher Education. *Standards for Professional Development Schools.* Washington, DC: Author, 2001.
Pilato, V. H., M. Dunkle, K. Fleming, and C. Wittmann. "Professional Development School Standards in Maryland." In *Implementing Pds Standards: Stories from the Field*, edited by M. Levine and R. Trachtman. Washington, DC: National Council for Accreditation of Teacher Education, 2005.
Teitel, L. *Assessing the Impacts of Professional Development Schools.* Washington, DC: American Association of Colleges for Teacher Education, 2000.
———. *How Professional Development Schools Make a Difference: A Review of Research.* revised, 2nd ed. Washington, DC: National Council for Accreditation of Teacher Education, 2004.
U.S. Department of Education. 2001. No Child Left Behind. In, http://nochildleftbehind .gov (accessed August 15, 2005).

Chapter Two

The Holmes Group:
A Vision for PDS Research

As new professional development schools are being created and existing ones seek to renew and sustain themselves, it is important to revisit the three seminal reports of The Holmes Group that set the expectations for research in PDS. In this chapter, the three reports—*Tomorrow's Teachers, Tomorrow's Schools, and Tomorrow's Schools of Education*—are reviewed with an emphasis on the principles, beliefs, values, and implications for inquiry and research in PDS. This review and discussion serves as background and reminder as to why PDS research is so vital to the overall school reform effort.

TOMORROW'S TEACHERS

The first report of The Holmes Group, *Tomorrow's Teachers*, addresses the need for a common vision toward the professionalization of teaching. A shared agenda that brings together universities, school districts, states, teachers unions and associations, and other partners includes five goals: (1) to make the education of teachers intellectually more solid; (2) to recognize differences in teachers' knowledge, skill, and commitment, in their education, certification, and work; (3) to create standards of entry to the profession—examinations and educational requirements—that are professionally relevant and intellectually defensible; (4) to connect institutions of higher education to schools; and (5) to make schools better places for teachers to work, and to learn (p.4).

However, in order to undertake such an agenda, constituents must have a common understanding of the obstacles involved. First, the notion that teaching is merely an act of transmitting information is outdated for the twenty-first century and beyond. The "stand and deliver" model of teachers' transmitting what they know and then, in turn, having students simply feed back that information can no longer be accepted for the training of teachers. Teaching must be interactive and candidates must learn new models of instruction that are research based and put students at the center of their teaching. Moreover, teachers should be empowered to make decisions on their students' behalf, thus suggesting some degree of professional autonomy for making curricular and other decisions (p.28). Next, institutions are unfit for teachers as professionals. Historically, teachers have been primarily young, single females who worked until they were married and then left teaching to raise families. Men have been in the minority in teaching and typically "moved up" to administrative positions, thus abandoning the classroom. With this constant turnover, teaching and teacher education have remained places designed for a youthful, short-term job market, rather than places that support those who would make teaching a career (p.33).

The idea of "career" assumes some differentiation within the profession. Historically, teachers in the U.S. have stayed in the classroom, typically with one group of students, and have been isolated from their peers. Advancement has been in the form of becoming a school administrator, taking a position in the district office, or earning a doctorate and moving to the university. Until the school reform movement of the 1980s, there were few positions that enabled teachers to continue working with students in some capacity and also included working with adults. *Tomorrow's Teachers* envisions a differentiated career structure that includes instructors (those who make a temporary commitment to teaching, have delineated roles and responsibilities, and are supervised); professional teachers (those who are certified as autonomous practitioners without supervision); and career professional teachers (those who possess the knowledge and skills for improving the educational effectiveness of other teachers).

Finally, demonstration sites must be created as contexts for the application and development of the new vision of the teaching profession. Much like a teaching hospital, the professional development school (PDS) is a new institution that brings together practicing teachers and administrators with university faculty in partnerships to improve practice for the benefit of students. The partners "provide superior opportunities for teachers and administrators to influence the development of their profession, and for university faculty to increase the professional relevance of their work, through (1) mutual deliberation on problems with student learning, and their possible solutions; (2) shared teaching in the university and schools; (3) collaborative research on the problems of educational practice; and (4) cooperative supervision of prospective teachers and administrators" (p. 56).

In order to accomplish the goals of *Tomorrow's Teachers*, a collective commitment to action is required for connecting schools to schools of education
in a substantive and sustained way. To this end, the principles of PDS include
values of reciprocity, experimentation, systematic inquiry (the careful testing
of new ideas) and student diversity (p. 67).

TOMORROW'S SCHOOLS

In the Preface of *Tomorrow's Schools* The Holmes Group emphasizes the universities' commitment *"to enhance the quality of schooling*, through research
and development and the preparation of career professionals in teaching"
(p. vii). Rather than offering a template that specifies the details of how a PDS
should be operationalized, the report includes six principles that serve as
launching points for negotiating with schools and districts interested in the
mutual work of PDS, thus making each partnership a unique context. The
principles for building tomorrow's schools provide the superstructure for
co-constructing the new institution where the teaching profession envisioned
in *Tomorrow's Teachers* will flourish.

First, the PDS is a learning community where teaching and learning for understanding are paramount. Curriculum is "a way of living and acting to make
sense of experience"(p. 10). It leads to understanding and ultimately links to
community (p. 11). The second principle, learning community, embraces
young and old, and meshes academics, citizenship, and life (p. 24) so that a
freedom of discourse rooted in respect and trust enables members "to think
powerfully and for a purpose" (p. 20). Educating everybody's children for
overcoming the educational and social barriers of an unequal society constitutes the third principle. Because the "seeds of failure for many children are
sown early" (p. 29), the PDS investigates the roots of failure to "create alternative ways of managing students' academic careers so that many more can
be captured by the ideas and habits of real learning" (p. 31). Thus, research
and theory in the PDS must be connected to issues of diversity, equity, and
social justice pertaining to all students regardless of their race, culture, language, academic ability, gender, and physical ability (p. 38). In sum, the PDS
respects the cultures of all its members by deliberately drawing their voices
and concerns into the mainstream of the learning community's life.

The fourth principle is that a PDS is a place for teaching adults as well as
children. PDS is better for children because all education professionals, including those who are learning to teach, are actively engaged in using best
teaching practices in a supportive and reflective environment. Ultimately,
children receive the benefit of improved instruction and assessment for con-

tinuous improvement of their learning. The PDS is better for student teachers because it directly bridges the gap between theory and practice. Student teachers are educated in a real world context of an existing school with all its challenges and rewards. In addition, the PDS is better for education school faculty and experienced teachers. "Two criticisms commonly leveled against the university are that the faculty who teach teachers are too far removed from the realities of schooling to provide knowledge that is usable; and that research on teaching and learning is too seldom based on actual contexts of schooling" (p. 50). The PDS context, however, allows university faculty, including those from arts and sciences who have always been involved in the schools, to "increase their opportunities to teach younger students and to work with teachers on curriculum, new forms of instruction, teacher preparation, and research" (p. 50). Finally, the PDS is better for school administrators because it provides a context for authentic learning about the art and craft of school administration rather than confining it to the university. The focus on professional development and collaboration for all educators in the PDS sets the stage for the emergence and growth of leadership within the new learning organization.

The fifth principle provides the basic premise for this book—that professional development schools are centers for reflection and inquiry. The ideas described in the previous principles "will be possible only in a school where purposeful preparation, mindful practice, critical reflection, mutual discourse, and continuing inquiry are normal ways of working, not exceptional events" (p. 55). By taking an inquiry stance together, schools and universities systematically look for ways to overcome the disconnections between research and practice across education institutions, thus benefiting schools and universities alike. Inquiry is a mutual task with "a common agenda for distributing knowledge and competence" (p. 59) that allows members to go beyond their bounds and work productively as a group. Inquiry in the PDS springs from school faculty's concerns about teaching and learning, thereby making it "more diverse than that arising from conventional canons of competent educational research" (p. 62). Inquiry and disciplined replication become the bases of school reform and put the potential for effecting change in the hands of faculty. This collective empowerment leads to multiple networks within and between partnerships as each generation of teachers supports the development of the next. In order to sustain such momentum, new forms of evaluation and rewards must be created so that all members will continue their commitment to the common enterprise.

Inventing a new organization is the sixth principle of *Tomorrow's Schools*. This is where the proverbial "rubber meets the road." As stated earlier, there is no template for creating a PDS. However, guideposts are offered to help direct a process for inventing the new organization. They include (1) coordinating instruction and services for children; (2) flexible staffing arrangements that address the needs of the school; (3) developing public forms of accountability, including setting standards for professionals; (4) balancing individual work with collaborative work; and (5) establishing reciprocity between the university and the school. The report concludes with some practical advice from member institutions of The Holmes Group on how to create a PDS, such as involving arts and sciences faculty, building capacity, and avoiding burnout, among others.

TOMORROW'S SCHOOLS OF EDUCATION

The Holmes trilogy is culminated by *Tomorrow's Schools of Education*, which was written in the midst of the standards movement. In this report teacher preparation institutions are challenged to make important changes in their curriculum, faculty, location of much of their work, and in their student body (p. 2). Better work and accountability can be attained when these changes are networked at the local, state, regional, and national levels (p. 3). In short, tomorrow's schools of education must undergo a transformation if they are to be a major force for professionalizing teaching and developing PDS as a part of school reform. Moreover, this transformation has special implications for educational research. In the past, research conducted by universities has given "short shrift to the study of teaching and learning as it is carried out in the public schools" (p. 11). In the new paradigm of collaboration with schools, however, "universities will have to redirect their investment in education R&D to take account of long-term applied work on what needs to be done to improve the public schools" (p. 11). Thus, one of the goals of the renewed school of education is to "make research, development, and demonstration of quality learning in real schools and communities a primary mission" (p. 13).

By taking a more proactive role in the greater educational debate, tomorrow's schools of education get down to the heart of the matter: knowledge development, professional development, and—especially as it pertains to the premise of this book—policy development. The development of policy should become a major item on the agenda of the education school. "Like their colleagues throughout the departments of the university who influence public policy on transportation, labor, housing, and health care, those who educate educators should similarly strive to bring their expertise to bear for the public good" (p. 24). Policy development could include "future directions in school finance, performance assessment, teacher testing and hiring" and could "oversee, pilot, and test versions of programs that might be studied as a prelude to legislation" (p. 25).

Making the commitment to policy development, however, is a major change for most teacher education institutions. Institutions that educate the largest numbers of educational professionals tend not to be research institutions but comprehensive master's universities or small liberal arts colleges whose mission is to prepare teachers. These institutions have excellent reputations in local school districts for working directly with teachers and schools both formally and informally, but when it comes to large-scale studies, assessments, and evaluations, research institutions are most likely to be called upon for assistance. Yet, the charge of *Tomorrow's Schools* challenges *all* schools of education to renew themselves, as appropriate to their individual missions, in order to become part of a collective force that addresses the compatibilities and incompatibilities of educational practice and policy (p. 39).

Through this collective work, all schools of education will ensure that all children can attain a certain level of education by developing policies for standards, equity and access, and coordination of services. This level of engagement assumes that institutions are willing to create the necessary structures, infrastructures, and mechanisms for doing the collaborative work. Human resources will be tantamount for carrying out the new mission and will require new accountability systems and reward structures. Finally, the work of the PDS, as envisioned in *Tomorrow's Schools,* becomes the work of schools of education in order to bring about substantial change in public schooling. The "PDS is no McDonald's franchise to be set in place ready to operate simply by acquiring the proper equipment and following the rules in a manual. Sweat and tears make the PDS. It is as much a process as a place, and its dynamism means that the PDS evolves constantly" (p. 79).

In brief, principles and beliefs for collaboration in research and inquiry are major factors for the creation, implementation, and sustainability of professional development schools as institutions of educational reform. Yet, attaining such a vision requires standards and guidelines for making the vision a reality. In Chapter Three, the Standards for Professional Development Schools established by the National Council for Accreditation of Teacher Education (NCATE) are reviewed and discussed as they pertain particularly to research and policy.

REFERENCES

"Tomorrow's Schools of Education: A Report of the Holmes Group." East Lansing, MI: The Holmes Group, 1995.

"Tomorrow's Schools: Principles for the Design of Professional Development Schools." East Lansing, MI: The Holmes Group, 1990.
"Tomorrow's Teachers: A Report of the Holmes Group." East Lansing, MI: The Holmes Group, 1986.

Chapter Three

The NCATE PDS Standards: Inquiry as Part of the Interwoven Fabric

One of the key concepts embedded in the NCATE PDS Standards is the integration of professional and student learning through inquiry, yet inquiry is often the function that receives the least attention in PDS work (p. 105). Although there is no research "standard" as such, all aspects of inquiry—developing questions, data gathering, analysis, assessment, self-assessment, reflection, evaluation, and collaborative decision-making for taking action—are interwoven in the PDS standards. Because inquiry in PDS is goal- and improvement-oriented and engages multiple partners in a multidimensional endeavor, assessing the outcomes of partnership work in a systematic way has been challenging and met with varying degrees of rigor and success.

The fact that PDS partnerships are developmental in nature adds to the challenge of conducting inquiry because partnership development can be uneven within any particular area (p. 108). The degree of commitment, level of expertise, degree of institutionalization and support, and impact the PDS has outside its partnering institutions can all add to the variation within a PDS, thus affecting its development. Ultimately, these variations have bearing on what types of research can be accomplished and the degree of quality therein. In this chapter, elements within each of the NCATE PDS Standards are reviewed, emphasizing the function of inquiry as a mechanism for change. (For a more detailed description of the NCATE PDS Standards, readers should access the document, *Standards for Professional Development Schools*, by either downloading it from http://www.ncate.org/public/pdsPub.asp?ch=140 or ordering the hard copy booklet directly from the National Council for Accreditation of Teacher Education).

STANDARD I: LEARNING COMMUNITY

The learning community of PDS has many implications for inquiry because it is "a learning-centered community that supports the integrated learning and development of P-12 students, candidates, and PDS partners through inquiry-based practice. PDS partners share a common vision of teaching and learning grounded in research and practitioner knowledge" (p. 11). The learning community embraces multiple partners. Members of P-12 schools and professional preparation programs are the principal members. Supporting members include the university, the school district, and the teachers associations or unions. Extended membership may include arts and sciences faculty, family and community members, and other individuals and organizations interested in the work of the collaborative.

First and foremost, the PDS *supports multiple learners*. This includes P-12 students, candidates, faculty, and other professionals in an integrated way. All members are learners regardless of their status, age, or previous experiences. *Work and practice are inquiry-based and focused on learning*, thus weaving together learning, accountability, and faculty development (p. 11). In addition, *inquiry is used routinely*, whether in individual classrooms, in departments, or across school-university levels. This, in turn, helps *develop a common shared professional vision of teaching and learning grounded in research and practitioner knowledge*. Ideally, "learning experiences and assessment processes in the PDS reflect the most current research and the most advanced wisdom of practitioners" (p. 12). Finally, the learning community *serves as an instrument of change*. As an outgrowth of the school and teacher preparation reform movement begun in the 1980s, the PDS is akin to the "common school" that ensures a solid foundation for all students for participating in a democratic society. Thus, partners integrate their knowledge and expertise to "develop new approaches for examining and improving the practices of individuals and the policies of both institutions" (p.12). As discussed elsewhere in this book, in order to reach the stage whereby inquiry can affect policy requires a high level of commitment and a solid and systematic agenda for research regardless of the partnership's length of existence or developmental stage.

STANDARD II:
ACCOUNTABILITY AND QUALITY ASSURANCE

Regarding this standard, PDS partners hold themselves accountable to each other and the public for "upholding professional standards for teaching and learning" (p. 13). There is collaboration for developing assessments, collecting information, and using results so that practices may be examined systematically. Outcome goals are established for P-12 students, teacher candidates, faculty, and other professionals. As mentioned above, the vision is to affect policies and practices at the local, state, and national levels through the new institution of the PDS.

PDS partners *develop professional accountability* by connecting their questions about learning for all members to the bigger mission, vision, and shared beliefs of the PDS. The process of asking and answering questions for the benefit of all sets the stage for a continuous improvement approach to partnership work, thus refining practices and increasing professionalism. These analyses are used to "make constructive changes at the individual, institutional, and partnership levels" (p. 13). PDS partners also *assure public accountability* by providing the public with evidence about what educators and students know and are able to do.

Together, PDS partners *develop assessments, collect information, and use results*. This accountability process ensures that individuals' practices and institutional policies will be responsive to the needs of P-12 students by building capacity within the organization. By "testing new ideas and questioning current norms and practices as they impact individual P-12 student achievement" (p. 14) teaching and learning are improved. Finally, the process of continuous assessment, reflection, and action employs multiple measures and multiple assessors for evaluating the growth of teacher candidates according to professional standards, and thus ensuring the quality of the teaching profession.

As an instrument of change, the school-university partnership must *engage with the PDS context* for attaining credibility in the eyes of its partners and other constituents. The partnership must fully explore the "who, what, when, where, how, and why" of its particular context. It "regularly examines the supports and constraints provided by the larger institutions and communities to which the PDS and the university are connected," for the purpose of aligning the work of the PDS with policies at the local, state, and national levels (p. 14).

STANDARD III: COLLABORATION

The standard for collaboration is based on the key assumption that PDS partners and partner institutions have made a commitment to each other in order to accomplish the mission of the partnership. Without this commitment, the level of inquiry and research needed to make changes in policy and practice cannot be attained. Outcomes for P-12 students, teacher candidates, teachers, university faculty, and other professionals cannot be improved without such commitment.

But how does this commitment manifest itself? First, the PDS partners *engage in joint work*. When truly working together (not just "cooperating") boundaries between institutions are blurred, thus destabilizing conventional lines of power and authority. This shake-up in power encourages fully integrated decision making "in areas that were formerly the sole domain of one of the partner institutions." (p. 15) Opportunities for continuous learning for children and adults are collaboratively designed and supported by improvement-oriented inquiries. Standards for participation and learning outcomes are determined together, and the broader education and policy communities are invited to engage in and critique the work.

Furthermore, partnerships *design roles and structures to enhance collaboration and develop parity*. Commitment to the joint work can be sustained for the long term when norms, roles, structures, and resource allocations are agreed upon by the partners and set in place. Partnership committees, including those focused on a research agenda, "include representatives from constituent groups and clearly define the expectations and responsibilities of partner institutions." Support structures, including those that provide incentives and rewards, are also agreed upon and set in place, thus enhancing the overall benefits of participation in the collaborative.

Finally, PDSs *systematically recognize and celebrate joint work and contributions of each partner*. This is especially meaningful in the area of inquiry and research because the traditional belief is that universities "do" research on schools with little regard for the imposition it makes on teachers, students, and administrators. However, when members work together to pursue a line of inquiry that is developmentally appropriate to the partnership, the process itself can become excellent professional development that is satisfying and cause for celebration by all.

STANDARD IV: DIVERSITY AND EQUITY

Collaboration for working on diversity and equity issues is also central to the mission of PDS. "PDS partners ensure that the policies and practices of the PDS partner institutions result in equitable learning outcomes for all PDS participants" (p. 16), thus reflecting one of the major tenets of PDS as conceived in the original Holmes Group's reports (see Chapter Two for more about the Holmes Group's focus on diversity and equity issues and their connections to inquiry). Equitable learning outcomes can occur when partnerships *ensure equitable opportunities to learn*. This can be attained when "PDS partners and candidates systematically analyze data to address the gaps in achievement among racial groups" (p. 16). By understanding and valuing the needs of its members, the PDS can increase its capacity for supporting students with exceptionalities and those who come from diverse racial, ethnic, gender, and socioeconomic groups. As part of the PDS's inquiry and research agenda, members *evaluate policies and practices to support equitable learning outcomes* and use "multiple and varied assessment approaches to measure learning" (p. 16). Finally, partner institutions *recruit and support diverse participants* and provide "academic, financial, and social support mechanisms to increase their success" (p. 16). In short, the PDS integrates the ideals of schooling in a democratic society.

STANDARD V: STRUCTURES, RESOURCES, AND ROLES

For the fifth standard, the PDS uses its authority to create structures, resources, and roles that support the learning community, provide ways and means for accountability and quality assurance, foster collaboration, and ensure diversity and equity. Governance structures not only oversee PDS roles and resources and communicate effectively with their partner institutions but also *ensure progress towards goals.* "The PDS partner institutions implement a process to evaluate needs and effectiveness in light of the PDS partnership's mission" (p. 17). Such an evaluation process assumes responsibility for utilizing the most current and informed knowledge about best practices in research. Yet, based on the analyses of PDS "research" described in Chapter Five, there is still a long way to go before all partnerships attain the levels of research that will have the greatest potential for effecting change. Without active governance structures, the PDS cannot undertake the breadth and depth of research required to make a difference at the local, state, and national levels.

REFERENCE

"Standards for Professional Development Schools." Washington, D.C.: National Council for Accreditation of Teacher Education, 2001.

Chapter Four

Analyses of PDS Research: Trends and Implications

A COMPARISON OF RESEARCH MODELS

From an examination of 18 years of professional development school publications (1988–2006), a framework for assessing the works emerged. This framework grew from the conception of PDS as a medical model of teacher preparation. As described previously in the introduction to this book, the medical model of educating doctors served as a model for PDS interaction between universities and schools. To that end, the model of medical research provides a protocol for research in education, particularly PDS. Twenty years prior to the inception of PDS, research in education began in earnest. During that same time, following WWII, research in medicine gained significant ground. Throughout this section of the chapter, stress on the parallel development and progression of research in education and medicine guides the discussion.

The shift in emphasis on science and mathematics education resulted from the effect of the launch of Sputnik by Russia in 1957. Political leaders, fearful that the country may be losing ground in the lead as a superpower, entreated scientists, mathematicians, psychologists, and educators to consider ways to change education in the United States to raise science and mathematics learning. Likewise, the medical field had learned many procedures, caring for men and women in WW II, as well as from concentration camp documentation and Japanese bomb victims. Doctors, scientists, and researchers in medicine worked to find treatments should the Cold War produce chemical, nuclear, and/or biological warfare uses. These two parallel worlds of phenomenology related to each other in the connection of the need for highly skilled scientists, doctors, and engineers to maintain security for the United States.

The two fields responded with careful consideration of the needs, resulting in research protocols in both fields. The educational response produced theoretical findings from the Woods Hole Conference, held in 1959 in Woods Hole, Massachusetts. Jerome Bruner, in his summary of the conference, *The Process of Education*, presented the spiral curriculum as an approach to teaching all concepts, to all learners. The medical community, following hundreds of years of theories about cancer, dating as far back as the 18th century, began researching breast cancer in earnest after WWII, in numerous medical schools around the world. By 1960, medical researchers isolated the Philadelphia Chromosome, the first genetic abnormality associated with a human cancer. Educational and medical research share some characteristics and there are differences that separate the two at a critical point, testing theory.

As noted in Figure 4.1, communities of researchers in both fields confront a phenomenon, a problem to solve. Both convene in conference formats to discuss the phenomenon under consideration and both may take years to define the parameters and consistent patterns. After years of idea exchange, theories as to the cause and possible approaches to solving the dilemma emerge. In the medical model of research, theories transform into hypotheses and scientific isolation of variability. To reveal possible solutions to the problem under study, the practice of isolating variability involves years, possibly decades of conscious work in laboratories and field trials. Following the rigorous demonstration of general public safety, a final scrutiny by governing agencies, the Food and Drug Administration (FDA) and others, approve treatment.

In the study of cancer, particularly breast cancer, the phenomenon increased in focus when more women were delivering babies and receiving obstetric care in medical facilities, as compared to prior to WW I and WW II. Ongoing discussions at American Medical Association meetings led to the "war on breast cancer." This resulted in a series of theories regarding the root cause, ways to isolate the cause, and the means by which to work toward care and possibly eradication of cancer. While the study of breast cancer seems foreign to a means of securing the nation, the phenomenon of breast cancer emerged, since so many women were available for study, due to the increase in women seeking medical care for deliveries of their children. The overall care of women led to more study of cancer among women. The findings from these studies support all cancer research and the need to overcome cancers resulting from possible outside biological and chemical warfare. Multiple theories regarding cancer emerged and pursued through intense research, in an effort to isolate contributing variables,

Figure 4.1.   The Relationship Between a Medical Model of Research and An Educational One

Medical Model of Research	Example	Educational Model of Research	Example
Phenomenon Recognized	Cancer as an example of what comes of chemical and biological warfare	Phenomenon Recognized	Sputnik as an example of scientific and mathematical superiority
Ideas for change	Extensive reports of widespread occurrence conveyed by doctors at meetings, centers for disease, etc. Call for theories as to why breast cancer flourishes	Ideas for change	Woods Hole Conference 1959 brought scientists, mathematicians, psychologists, etc together to consider the relationship between schooling and scientific prowess in the cold war. Discussions of why education has failed to create better scientists and mathemeticians
Theoretical positions	Diet, estrogen levels, stress, chemical imbalance	Theoretical positions	Spiral curriculum can provide a path for learning any scientific or mathematical idea incrementally
Testing the theory	Funded research in medical schools and hospitals to isolate the cause and test treatment protocols	Application of the theory, with minimal testing, rare isolation of variability	The spiral curriculum has been applied and adhered to as practice since the early 1960s
Conclusions	Examine the results of the treatments and re-assess; implement wholesale after years of study, testing and FDA approvals	Inconclusive results	Spiraling the curriculum in the form of national and state standards persists; uncontested

which led to the means by which to possibly cure, prevent, and/or eradicate cancer. Though cancer remains a phenomenon, the rate of recovery, cure, and eradication has increased as a result of theory testing, isolation of variability, experimental work, and painstaking research, which has been scrutinized and vetted through national agencies, all of which are documented in medical research journals.

Educational researchers left the Woods Hole conference with a mandate to find ways to create meaningful mathematics and science instruction in the schools. Jerome Bruner, a psychologist charged with preparing the final report for the conference, asserted that the findings and theoretical positions posed as a result of the conference required careful experimentation and testing in school settings. He introduced several theories of education, including his own theory of structured learning, otherwise known as the spiral curriculum. His theory purported that any child could learn anything at any age if the concept were structured in a way that made it accessible to the learner. A 20–year review (1960–1980) of spiral curriculum theory reveals a discussion of the implementation of spiral curriculum across multiple disciplines. However, scientific study of the theoretical position on spiral curriculum did not materialize following the implementation of the theory into practice. Instead, the leap from phenomenon to theory to wholesale practice circumvents the isolation of variability of whether the theory of spiral curriculum differs significantly from other approaches to organizing the curriculum. In essence, no recovery, cure, and/or eradication of the problem of falling behind resulted.

Twenty-one years later, under President Reagan, Secretary of Education Terrell Bell formed the National Commission on Excellence in Education. The commission created *The Nation At Risk* report in 1983. This report generally condemned public education, claiming mediocrity as the result and root of the problem. Ronald Reagan alleged that to solve these ills in schools, school prayer, vouchers, and abolition of the department of education should ensue. A number of universities responded differently. A consortium of leading universities that touted the value of education programs, particularly teacher preparation programs, at the university level met to discuss ways to salvage and promote reform for teacher education programs, giving rise to The Holmes Group in 1986. The Holmes Group set forth proposals to reform and revive public education through collaborative connections between schools and universities that interface in the venue of teacher preparation (see Chapter Two in this book for a summary of The Holmes Group's reports).

The subsequent reports (1986, 1990, and 1995), wending their way into the literature, created the PDS movement, another phenomenon in U.S. education. From the inception of the theory of PDS, the literature has been rife with commentary regarding the implementation, research limitations to university faculty, building community, articulated developments of the model, and descriptions of PDS programs in elementary, middle, and high schools across the United States.

ANALYSES OF PDS RESEARCH

An electronic database search in EBSCO host resulted in 942 titles with the search title "professional development schools." Titles perused for the by-words "professional development schools, PDS, or partnerships" were included in a review-pool of 450 articles. Abstracts of these 450 articles, reviewed for two elements: (1) method of research and (2) concepts researched, yielded trends in PDS publications, between 1988–2006. The selection of articles for analysis found basis in the desire to isolate PDS specific study. While many teacher preparation programs engage in PDS work, the study of its effect on advancing the teaching profession and student achievement remains illusive in the literature. The purpose of this book is to consider the study of PDS and advance the use of accepted methods of research to achieve the advancement of the teaching profession through PDS preparation, to the attainment of higher student achievement, while working in collaborative work. Consequently, all studies found in the literature not specifically mentioning PDS, partnerships, or professional development schools were not considered for this review.

Methods of Research

For the purposes of classifying the method of research, the eight AERA supported methods of research: arts-based, historical, philosophical, ethnographic, case study, survey, comparative experimental, and quasi-experimental served as initial identifiers (see Chapter Five for a brief description of the various methods). As the review progressed, four additional categories emerged: literature/ book reviews, reports, descriptions of programs (stories), and ideas. Placement of publications into categories followed several identification procedures. All abstracts clearly delineating the method employed found placement in the articulated category. Abstracts without clearly stated methods were examined for additional information that led to the classification of the publications. Data sources and analyses described in the abstracts provided additional cues as to the methods employed in the studies as well as thematic content. Abstracts describing the use of multiple forms of data, such as interview, observation, record examination, and/or journal entries to depict a single PDS setting, classroom, or course, were placed in the classification of case study. When no specific data were noted and the abstract stated clearly that the publication described the setting, the publication was classified as description. Abstracts specifically delineating literature searches fell directly into the literature review category. Some articles spoke to the "notion" of PDS and the value of it, without earmarking a functioning PDS program. These publications were placed into the category of ideas. Finally, all abstracts were identified by year of publication.

The data were organized for analysis to yield trends: across years, within each year, and across research methods. The nominal data analyses constituted frequency counts and percentages. In spite of this simple statistical procedure, results point to patterns in PDS research that can be used to inform and guide future research decisions in PDS. Results generally follow the trend of previous educational research conducted following the Woods Hole conference, to describe the theory of PDS in practice as prescribed by the theories put forth by The Holmes Group. However, in the review of PDS studies, a slight trend toward empirical methods, mostly qualitative, but some quantitative, became apparent.

Trends Across Years

Across all years, 1988–2006, patterns of submission emerged across two time periods. The majority of articles reviewed were published between 1997 and 2002, representing 54 percent of the published articles. Twenty-six percent of the articles reviewed were found in years 1991 and 1994. These two groupings of dates represent 80 percent of the articles reviewed. Between 1991–1994, 78 percent of the studies were represented by the categories of *descriptions/stories, ideas about PDS, and case studies*. This trend continued in the 1997–2002 studies, with *case study, description/stories, and ideas*, plus *survey* contributing to 79 percent of the studies reviewed. In both groups, *description/stories from the field* between 1991 and 1994 constituted 39 percent of the articles reviewed, while this trend diminished to 34 percent between 1997 and 2002. *Ideas articles* contributed 28 percent of the studies in the earlier group, whereas this figure was diminished to 14 percent in the later years. *Case studies* in the earlier trend group constituted 10 percent of the total group, but increased to 18 percent in the later trend group.

The strongest trend difference in the two year-groups was the influx of *survey research* in the later years' group of articles. Between 1991–1994 *survey studies* constituted only 8 percent of the total studies during this era. In contrast, the number of *survey studies* grew to 13 percent between 1997–2002. This growth in survey research indicates a trend toward numeric means of ascertaining constituent perception and disposition regarding PDS. Results of

surveys serve as precursors to rigorous research involving other research
methods that investigate the PDS setting more deeply. Survey results define
the position of constituents and aid the researcher in making decisions regarding agendas that investigate through ethnography, quasi, and experimental designs.

An analysis across the 18 years of PDS publication revealed interesting trends
in research and non-research methods. Research methods included the eight
sanctioned and supported by AERA. Non-research methods included the four
previously articulated. The trends observed in the 450 publications reviewed revealed that 68 percent of the publications regarding PDS revealed *non-research
methods*. Of these, 51 percent were *descriptions of programs. Literature reviews*
constituted 10 percent, while *reports*, and *ideas* about PDS, consisted of 9 and
31 percent of the remaining studies reviewed. The trend in non-research articles
across the 18 years of the phenomenon of PDS suggests that descriptions in
the form of *stories, reports, literature reviews, and idea sharing* bear out the
phenomenon of PDS in a well documented, non-research based format. These
descriptions, reports, literature reviews, and idea generations provide the foundation for guiding future research-based agendas.

The remaining 40 percent of the publications reviewed showed trends toward
primarily *qualitative approaches* to research from the eight prescribed by
AERA. Among the six qualitative methods, *case studies* dominated with 35 percent of the 40 percent of the research-based publications reviewed. The other
qualitative approaches, *arts based, historical, philosophical, and ethnographi-
cal*, represented zero, 6, 4, and 1 percent of the qualitative studies reviewed, respectively. The implication from these figures suggests that *case study* is a fa-
vored approach to research of PDS. This trend relates directly to the story telling
or descriptions of programs noted in non-research based studies. However, case
study more explicitly probes into the PDS setting, employing multiple means by
which to describe the program under study, whereas the description/story describes the situation from a single lens of the author, without the depth of probing afforded by the multiple forms of data analyzed in case study methodology.
The lack of use of other AERA endorsed qualitative methods suggests a lack of
knowledge or skill in the use of these methods.

Three quantitative methods, *survey, quasi-experimental, and experimental*,
represented approximately one third of the 40 percent of the research-based
publications. *Survey method* represented 26 of the original 40 percent of all
articles. Due to the methods used to examine the history of research across
the last 18 years, abstract analysis, there was no way to determine validity,
reliability, return rate, and quality of the surveys issued and reported. *Quasi-
experimental methods* represented 6 percent of the original 40 percent. *No
experimental studies* were noted, as defined by Campbell and Stanley. The

purpose of this examination, to account for methods, precludes the in depth look at research quality.

The use of survey research indicates a convenient means by which to chronicle the perceptions and dispositions of multiple PDS constituents. This basic research leads to decisions regarding other more carefully controlled, quantitative studies of PDS. However, to accomplish quasi and experimental work in PDS, high levels of trust among university and school personnel are required. For schools to agree to random selection or even matched groups for study of the effect of PDS on student achievement, in the current climate of meeting No Child Left Behind (NCLB) and Adequate Yearly Progress (AYP) expectations, high levels of trust must be established. Years of descriptions of PDS programs indicate that change in university personnel, particularly in light of additional pressures to publish in highly competitive journals, restricts the potential for building trust. Due to the perception that PDS offers a limited research agenda, university personnel seek other agendas, resulting in the exacerbation of descriptions/stories about PDS programs (see the discussion of The Holmes Group's charge for PDS research in Chapter Two of this book). While these stories are valuable to all PDS researchers seeking knowledge of how other programs work, more rigorous methods would reveal the *effectiveness* of PDS regarding teacher preparation and student achievement.

Trends Within Years

Eras of PDS Development

Each year of PDS publications reviewed indicated mixed trends both in terms of methods and salient topics. The summary of the review is done in groups of years. The first group represents the *beginning* of PDS when it was forming itself, 1988–1990. The second group represents the *growing* years, when PDS programs were growing and reporting their growth, 1991–1994. The third group represents the *functioning* years, 1995–2000, when PDS settings were working to establish and maintain. The final group, the years of *accountability*, 2001–2006, finds PDS under scrutiny by multiple agents including, but not exclusive of: NCATE, USDOE (NCLB), state agencies, and local school district agencies. Publications within each era represent the authors' perspectives of the era.

Salient Topics

Salient topics were determined by using four basic questions to screen the abstracts. The first was, what is PDS and who is involved? This category described *general guiding principles and philosophy, conceptual frameworks, and models*, and included *descriptions of roles and resources* needed for applying the ideas. The second was, how are power and control negotiated to create the new institution of PDS? This category included emphases on *collaboration and restructuring*. The third was, where do PDSs operate? This category focused on *context* and included topics about *change and experimentation, geographic locations and networks*, and *subject matter focus or curriculum*. The fourth category was, what are the impacts on constituents (the "so what" question) and included topics related to *accountability*, such as *assessment and evaluation, inquiry and problem solving*, and *policy and standards*.

Beginning Era: 1988–1990

During this era, the 18 articles reviewed, revealed a trend representative of its title, the beginning. Eleven articles fell into the category of ideas and philosophy. This logical collection represents the importance of publications that inform and build a theoretical basis for the development of the phenomenon PDS. Four of the articles told the story of established programs in the beginning stages. Again, this important description provides PDS researchers interested in forming PDS programs the needed information to begin to plan and develop research agendas. Finally, during this era three other studies, with one in each category—report, survey, and case study—indicate that early work in the practice was under way.

Growing Era: 1991–1994

During this era, an escalation of *research-based studies* was noted in the article pool. Of the 118 articles reviewed, 11 *case studies*, eight *survey studies*, and three *philosophic articles* became apparent. The trend continued in the areas of *non-research*, as was noted in the 36 *ideas* and 46 *description/story* articles reviewed. This era marked growth in the number of articles and the increased use of traditional research methods. In spite of this development, substantial articles fell within the non-research categories, suggesting a continued need to tell the story of programs, while developing additional views about the phenomenon. Nearly two thirds of the articles contained descriptions of *conceptual frameworks* and various *contexts* for PDS. The remaining articles were focused on restructuring efforts for new *collaborations* between schools and universities or reconceptualizing previously established professional development networks to include a PDS model. This era marks less than the ten year mark of the phenomenon, and therefore, the types of non-research based publications seem somewhat reasonable in the continued development of the concept of PDS.

Functioning Era: 1995–2000

This third era, 1995–2000, began a second decade of PDS study and research. The appearance of ten *reports*, nine *historical studies*, and five *quasi-
experimental studies* suggests that the PDS phenomenon had taken hold and
was functioning. This era showed an increase in the number of articles from
118 to 192. Within that increase, 27 articles represented *case study* research
and 26 represented *survey* research. These numbers represent 50 percent of
the total number of articles in the pool for this era, indicating that PDS research had begun an inclination toward research-based methods. The remaining articles represented *descriptions/stories* of programs and *ideas* about
PDS, with 46 and 35 articles respectively. The tendency in the first part of the
second decade implied that the PDS program was functioning prepared to
study itself employing higher levels of scrutiny. This implication is also supported by the finding that nearly half the articles focused on *assessing the impacts* of PDS, especially as it related to the *learning community*, a term frequently found in the abstracts from this era. In addition, about one third of the
publications about *assessment* focused on assessing *frameworks* and *restructuring* efforts. On the other hand, only 7 percent of the publications in this era
focused on issues concerning *policies and standards* and a mere 3 percent on
issues of *diversity and equity*. Of note, 10 percent of the articles included
some type of *comparison*, thus suggesting that "PDS" was gradually being
viewed as an intervention with measurable parameters.

Accountability Era: 2001–2006

With the advent of No Child Left Behind, the introduction of the NCATE
PDS Standards, accountability on the minds of state legislators, and fear in
the hearts of many local school administrators and teachers, scrutiny of PDS'
effectiveness to bring about change in teacher preparation and student
achievement increased. In answer to the charge from the U. S. Department of
Education for experimental research in schools, an examination of this era of
PDS research yields only six *quasi-experimental* studies, with no indication
of experimental work. In addition, during this era marked a lessening of the
number of studies from 192 to 123. Among the *research-based* articles, *case
study* and *survey* were represented with 25 and 13 articles, respectively.
Among *the non-research based* articles, *descriptions/stories*, *reports*, *literature reviews*, and ideas were represented by 43, 8, 10, and 15 articles, respectively, with more than half the total articles of the era continuing to focus on
the *description of the context*. This research answer among the 123 articles
considered, implies a disregard or delayed reaction to the era's purpose even

though more than half the topics included some type of *assessment of impacts*, especially those focused on the *context* of PDS. Approximately one fourth of the articles included some aspect of *assessing frameworks and restructuring efforts*, a slight decrease from that found in the previous era. Nine percent of the publications included a focus on *policy and standards* issues and 2 percent on issues of *diversity and equity*. With the age of PDS approaching 20 years and the increase in pressure to demonstrate effectiveness, the research fails to demonstrate the strength of the phenomenon. With over 61 percent of the articles falling into the category of *non-research* during this era, the field of research in PDS demonstrates a need to examine its trajectory of research and find common ground with the expectations from external audiences, particularly to those who consider teacher preparation suspect.

Trends Across Methods

As noted previously, the trend across methods of research showed tendencies toward non-research approaches in the areas of program descriptions/stories, literature review, reports, and ideas, which are not necessarily philosophically based. From a thematic perspective, the trend showed tendencies toward examinations of the context of PDS, including the learning community, which incorporated some dimension of assessing the outcomes of the context as well as describing it. Up until the third era of PDS research the trends in research, beginning with ideas, philosophy, and descriptions/stories, grew into research-based approaches, until the final era of accountability, where only 40 percent of the articles analyzed represented research-based methods. Yet, by the third era, more than half the articles—as purported in their abstracts—were focused on assessment. This seeming backward movement suggests a need for a framework for creating and supporting research agendas for undergraduate and graduate students, university faculty, and school personnel, to verify and justify the value of PDS methods of teacher preparation as viable in a world of educational accountability. The tenets of this book provide such a framework and protocol for a research agenda. In Chapters Six to Nine, the development of the framework provides a rationale for increasing the use of research-based methods and diminishing non-research based practices.

REFERENCES

Armstrong, Jenny. "Curricular and Instructional Factors Which Facilitate Mathematical Learning." *Journal of Experimental Education* 38, no. 2 (1969): 5–15.

Barnes, Henry. "An Introduction to Waldörf Education." *Teachers College Record* 81 no. 3 (1980): 323–36

Bruner, Jerome. *The Process of Education.* Cambridge, Mass: Harvard University Press, 1965.

Campbell, Donald, and Julian Stanley. *Experimental and Quasi-Experimental Designs for Research.* Chicago, Ill: Rand McNally and Co., 1963.

Carter, D. A. "Mathematics in Middle Schools." *Mathematics in School* 5, no. 3 (1976): 2–9.

Cowan, P, H Morrison, and F McBride. "Evidence of a Spiral Curriculum Using a Mathematical Problem-Solving Tool." *Interactive Learning Environments* 6, no. 3 (1998).

Education, National Commission for Excellence in. "A Nation at Risk: The Imperative for Educational Reform (No. 455–B-2)." edited by United States Department of Education. Washington, D.C.: United States Department of Education, 1983.

Fried, Michael N, and Miriam Amit. "A Spiral Task as a Model for in-Service Teacher Education." *Journal of Mathematics Teacher Education* 8, no. 5 (2005): 419–36.

The History of Cancer. Accessed January 2007. In, The American Cancer Society. (accessed).

Holsberry, Carmen. "Secondary School Literature Curriculum Design: A Multifunctional Approach." *Clearing House* 52 no. 7 (1979): 313–17.

Lawrence, C. M. "A Complete Program of Agricultural Education." *Agriculture Education Magazine* 42, no. 1 (1969): 5.

Leichter, Hope. "A Note on Time and Education." *Teachers College Record* 81 no. 3 (1980): 360–70

Lerner, Barron H. *The Breast Cancer Wars: Hope, Fear, and the Pursuit of a Cure in Twentieth-Century America.* New York: Oxford University Press, 2001.

Malik, Alam Sher, and Rukhsana Hussain Malik. "Core Curriculum and Special Study Modules at the Faculty of Medicine and Health Sciences, Universiti Malaysia Sarawak." *Education for Health: Change in Learning & Practice* 17, no. 3 (2004): 292–302.

McAnarney, Harry E. "Whither the Elementary School Science Program?" *Science Education* 53, no. 3 (1969): 237–39.

Murphy, Patricia. "Modules for Consumer Education: A Spiral-Process Approach to Curriculum Development." *American Vocational Journal* 48, no. 7 (1973): 52.

O'Donnell, John F. "The New English." *Greater Philadelphia Council of Teache rs of English Newsletter* 6 no. 1 (1968): 10–7.

Pandolfi, R. "Career Education at the Elementary School Level: Preparation for the Future." *Man/Society/Technology* 33, no. 7 (1974.): 206–8.

Pogonowski, Lenore. "A Personal Retrospective on the Mmcp." *Music Educators Journal* 88 no. 1 (2001): p. 4–27.

Reavis, Charles A., and Frank R. Whittacre. "Professional Education of Teacher: A Spiral Approach." *Peabody Journal of Education* 46, no. 5 (1969): 259–64.

"Tomorrow's Schools of Education: A Report of the Holmes Group." East Lansing, MI: The Holmes Group, 1995.

"Tomorrow's Schools: Principles for the Design of Professional Development Schools." East Lansing, MI: The Holmes Group, 1990.

"Tomorrow's Teachers: A Report of the Holmes Group." East Lansing, MI: The Holmes Group, 1986.

Trumper, Ricardo. "Teaching About Energy through a Spiral Curriculum: Guiding Principles." *Journal of Curriculum and Supervision* v12, no. n1 (1996): p. 66–75.

Wilson, Robert D. "Bilingual Education for Navajo Students." *National Association of Student Personnel Admininistration* 6, no. 4 (1969): 65–69.

Chapter Five

A Framework Using AERA Research Methods and NCATE PDS Standards

An AERA publication, *Contemporary Methods for Research in Education* outlines eight methods of research in education. Five of the methods (arts-based, historical, philosophic, ethnographic, and case study) require knowledge and skill in qualitative research and analysis. Survey research necessitates psychological competence in creating stem items that ascertain self-reported information that represents the nature of the phenomenon under study. Whereas, quasi-experimental and experimental methods entail knowledge and skills in quantitative data collection and analysis. Historical research has more recently included quantitative methods that include data analysis of trends in educational testing and the historical implications for future decisions. The brief description of each method that follows provides PDS partnership researchers with the tools necessary to make decisions regarding their level of knowledge and skill in using different research methods. Later in the chapter, a discussion of a framework for method selection, based on PDS developmental levels, provides additional guidance. No matter the method, the protocol of good research remains constant: establish the purpose, problem, setting, investigators, and methods; excellence in research will follow.

ARTS-BASED RESEARCH

Arts-Based Research, according to Barone and Eisner constitutes seven features: (1) creation of virtual reality, (2) presence of ambiguity, (3) use of expressive language, (4) use of contextualized or vernacular language, (5) promotion of empathy, (6) personal signature of researcher/writer, and (7) presence of aesthetic form . While the authors articulate each in detail, they also point out that all seven are not required to constitute excellence in arts-based research; however, the more that are incorporated, the more artistic the design. The most prominent forms of arts-based research are educational criticism and narrative storytelling. In educational criticism researchers use description, interpretation, evaluation and thematics to provide an aesthetic perspective of the educational phenomenon. Narrative researchers "describe lives and tell stories of them, write narratives of experience." In both forms, the seven features guide the researcher through the process of applying arts-based research protocol.

HISTORICAL RESEARCH

The work of researchers employing historical methods includes the study of the educational phenomenon from the perspective of the people, situations, and related past events and their combined influence on the present and future. Historical researchers review documents, interview stakeholders past and present, examine physical settings, and create a sense of time, place, and sequence of events. This translates to implications for future decisions. Recently, some historical researchers turned to quantitative methods for data collection, using attendance, test scores, population shifts, etc., to define the historical trends in education. In either form, the historical researcher not only tells the story of time past but infers future development. The purpose extends beyond the need to know what went before, to how history influences and guides future decisions.

PHILOSOPHIC RESEARCH

Maxine Green, prominent philosophic researcher, indicates that philosophic research searches for understanding and interpretation, rather than explanation and prediction and control. Researchers applying philosophic methodology employ the tenets of hermenuetics; the science and methodology of interpreting texts; the science of interpreting concepts, theories, and principles. The philosophic researcher participates in the environment of education and creates meaning of observed events. The relevance of epistomological, metaphysical, and axiological problems within an educational setting fuels the philosophic research to deeply probe the questions of the nature of the universe, how we know what we know, and the aesthetic and ethical underpinnings of observations. Philosophic researchers create meaning from experience and continue to ask questions, rather than provide answers.

ETHNOGRAPHIC RESEARCH

Ethnography, an anthropological field of research, when applied to education, studies the ethnic/cultural aspects of an educational setting. Ethnographers undergo a particular process to create their products of cultural understanding of the "way of life of an identifiable group of people." The ethnographic researcher learns about and represents with clarity the deeper understanding of the culture under study, creating a human perspective of the phenomenon. To achieve this, ethnographic researchers embed themselves in the culture at varying stages from observer, to participant observer, to interviewer, to participant, while chronicling the lives of people and how their interactions form an understanding of the culture in which they operate and how their interactions form the culture. Throughout, the researcher uses multiple data sources and record keeping methods to create a rich understanding of the culture.

CASE STUDY RESEARCH

A case study researcher focuses on "one person, one classroom, one curriculum, one case." In case studies, multiple forms of data inform the study of the "one." Researchers observe, analyze documents, interview, survey, and in general, come to understand the one case in its entirety from multiple perspectives. Action research, the personal case study, implies similar methods of using multiple data sources to further the understanding of a single person's educational situation within the context of a person living the research through their immediate actions in the educational setting. The principle of using multiple data sources applies in action research. Whether through the eyes of an outside observer or an action researcher, subsequent to the study of the case, the researcher tells the story of the people, events, and place under study, combining all the data sources to create the image of the "one." Often, in the circumstance of action research, the researcher uses the results to determine personal change or affirmation of practice.

SURVEY RESEARCH

"The purpose of survey research is to describe specific characteristics of a large group of persons, objects, or institutions." Jaeger suggests that survey researchers hold three characteristics in common: (1) interest in specific facts, (2) groups are well defined, and (3) a desire to know about the present conditions of the group. Inherent in survey research is the sampling required to provide verification that findings tendered represent the group. Survey researchers understand and apply well defined sampling techniques: stratified random samples, sample size, sample statistics, and while obtaining a large percentage of survey returns. Adherence to these techniques validates and strengthens the results of the research. Construction of survey items requires an understanding of the complexity of item design that ascertains the present conditions and characteristics of the group surveyed. Forms of survey include: mailers, telephone, face-to-face interviews, and more recently, web-basesd programs. Assuring returns in the range of 60–80 percent challenges the best of researchers. However, returns much lower than this figure brings into question the value of acquired information as representative of the group under study.

COMPARATIVE EXPERIMENTAL RESEARCH

To study the effect of an educational intervention on change in an educational setting, comparative experimental research provides the most powerful method. In a comparative experimental study, the researcher randomly selects groups of subjects from a given population and assigns groups to different forms of intervention, generally treatment and non-treatment, placebo group. Following the intervention, some form of test, related to the intervention, is administered to all groups to determine differences among the groups and within the groups on the phenomenon under study. This method accounts for concerns for internal and external validity and provides a level of confidence that the results represent true differences based on the intervention, rather than a selection or other form of bias. While this is powerful and the recommended form of research of the *No Child Left Behind* legislation, in educational settings the ethics of randomly selecting for treatment, when no child can be left behind, creates a conflict of purpose. To overcome this, researchers can offer treatment for all in need by administering the treatment at two different times while maintaining random selection.

QUASI-EXPERIMENTAL RESEARCH

As in the case of comparative experimental research, the quasi-experimental method applies the principles of intervention to groups representing independent samples of a population with a dependent variable used to test differences. The greatest difference lies with the selection of independent groups. In quasi-experimental designs independent groups are selected for spurious reasons, rather than random ones. Subjects volunteer to participate in a study and matched groups are arranged, then treatment administered to groups accordingly. An interrupted time-series design uses consistent collection of data at specific times during the study, allowing the researcher to establish trends across time as treatment is administered. Other time-series designs include single group, operant, miltiple group single, interaction, reversal, stratified multiple group, and sequential multiple group. In the quasi-experimental method, the subjects are not randomly selected, so the control for external and internal validity strain the reliability of the results, rendering the findings in this form of research less compelling than the comparison experimental method.

Partnerships in professional development schools, under pressure to account for the effectiveness of their programs regarding teacher preparation, student achievement, and a myriad of other accountability issues mandated by local, state, and national entities, need some means by which to study effectiveness. While the NCATE PDS Standards suggest the use of inquiry to address these accountability issues, prescription for approach to researching the phenomenon remains illusive. In this chapter, the relationship between the call for inquiry in the NCATE document and the appropriate methodology aligned with the levels of PDS partnership development are presented as a framework. The intention for creating the framework is to empower PDS workers at all levels to conduct appropriate research, therefore providing local, state, and national organizations with accountability required. In addition, well-developed and implemented research, when published, provides the field with in depth knowledge and understanding that informs the field and encourages growth and increased research through duplicated studies.

A FRAMEWORK FOR A DEVELOPMENTAL APPROACH FOR RESEARCH ON PDS

The framework for a developmental approach couples the aspects of the NCATE PDS Standards with the protocols and expectations of AERA recommended research methods. The framework's inception began with a word analysis of the NCATE PDS developmental stages to determine the defining elements and functional limits of each stage. Emergent verbs, defining the operationalization of each developmental stage, provided the initial framework for determining connections between NCATE PDS Standards and AERA research protocols (see Figure 5.1).

While the framework provides a vision of research possibilities, it does not limit the PDS researcher to these recommendations. Instead, the framework conveys a guide for PDS researchers to examine their PDS's developmental

**Figure 5.1. Connections between NCATE PDS Standards and
AERA Research Protocols**

NCATE PDS Developmental Standing	Recommended Research Approaches
Beginning	case study, survey, and historical
Developing	ethnography, survey, case study (including action research), history, quasi-experimental, and philosophic
At Standard	Primarily quasi-experimental and experimental; but inclusive of case study, survey, historical, and philosophic
Leading	case study, survey, historical, and philosophic

level and current research practice with an eye toward systemized, methodologically based research agendas.

An analysis of the language employed to describe the 22 elements affiliated with the Beginning Stage revealed several strong trends. The active verbs used in the portrayal of the Beginning PDS program emphasized several areas of characterization. The language describes a group of constituents who are forming their collaborative through planning and exploration and are expressing their mission and vision. The operative verbs in this standard support the designation of the NCATE Beginning stage as a formative stage, suggesting a time when the PDS program under review is forming its partners into a collaborative.

BEGINNING STAGE

In essence, the beginning stage of PDS program implementation involves *planning, articulating, exploring, and envisioning.* Specifically, the Beginning stage description states that, "Beliefs, verbal commitments, plans, organization and initial work are consistent with the mission of PDS partnerships. This means that even at the earliest stage of development PDS partners are committed to the key concepts of PDSs and their earliest work addresses how to take initial steps in that direction." The verbs *planning, articulating, exploring, and envisioning* imply establishing or the process of establishing a PDS program. Partners at this developmental stage begin to create meaning for themselves and for future involvement by other constituents. Fundamentally, a foundation built on shared vision and mission sets the stage for planning and exploring the potential for the PDS program. This understanding channels research initiatives.

Research recommendations for the beginning PDS, include: philosophic, case study, survey, and historical. These four methods provide PDS researchers in beginning PDS settings with tools to study a forming group as it builds relationships of trust and collaboration. An outside observer at the beginning stage can ascertain, while applying these four methods, the formation of the collaborative as it goes through the process of materializing. The data sources, with the exception of survey, elicited through observation and document analysis, inform but do not impede the process of relationships/ collaboration building. Survey research can be non-intrusive, if conducted with anonymity. In contrast, ethnographic, artistic, quasi-experimental, and experimental, require established levels of trust that facilitate the acquisition of more specific and pesonal data necessary to answering the questions studied employing these four methods.

DEVELOPING STAGE

At the developing stage, partners are pursuing the mission of the PDS partnership and there is evidence of partial institutional support. At the developing stage, partners are engaged in PDS work in many ways. However, their supporting institutions have not yet made changes in their policies and practices that would provide evidence of institutionalization. Partnerships at this level have found agreement on the mission and the work of connecting candidates with mentor teachers in a meaningful way. In addition, within the rubrics of the standards, recommendations for action research and planned observations of shared practice enter into this developmental stage. Finally, changes in instructional practices of university personnel also appear in this developmental stage.

Multiple research questions surface when considering the developing stage. Relationships, change, and the management of these emerge. With the collaborative more clearly defined and embraced by partners, the options for research increases due to the availability of data sources that follows increased trust. Different research methods appropriate at this developmental stage include: ethnography, survey, case study (including action research), history, quasi-experimental, and philosophic. The original four from the beginning stage continue at the developing stage but take on a more in depth form as deeper probing is possible when trust has been established.

An important aspect of the developing stage is the empowerment of more constituents, particularly mentor teachers. Mentor teachers serve as gatekeepers in each stage as they interface with university interns and students in the schools. The potential for research among teachers abounds at the developing stage. This is a ripe opportunity for university personnel to unite with teachers in action research projects. The level of risk involved in conducting action research projects suggests an amount of caution on the part of university personnel, eager to demonstrate the effect of PDS on student achievement. Teachers, often fearful of research, have to embody a sense of ownership of the research and should be supported as they traverse through the process of self-examination and outside scrutiny by others, a bi-product of action research.

At the developing stage, quasi-experimental design enters as a potential method of research. While teachers and principals may be willing to volunteer to participate in a study of effect, it is unlikely that they would be willing to accept a fully random selection of classes, students, and teachers for study of effect. Consequently, the quasi-experimental design approaches the need to determine the level of effect of PDS on student achievement, one of the expectations set in the NCATE PDS Standards at this stage of development. Even with a quasi-experimental design, the potential for halo effects and interference abound, consequently caution should be taken when designing using this method.

AT STANDARD STAGE

The at standard stage represents a fully functioning PDS program with an established mission integrated into the partnering institutions. PDS work is expected and supported, and it reflects what is known about best practices. At this stage partners work together effectively, resulting in positive outcomes for all learners. Partnering institutions have made changes in policies and practices that reflect what has been learned through PDS work and support PDS participants in meaningful ways. At this stage partners synchronize thought and function on a very high level, with an increased awareness of all learners and effect PDS has on their gains as learners. In addition, the support required to sustain and advance the program suggest a high functioning program. Finally, at this stage, policy change to support PDS beckons a very clear research objective.

Research possibilities at this stage encompass all recommended methods. The effect of programming on "positive outcomes" of all learners suggests, beyond the qualitative methods previously applied, quantitative methods of quasi-experimental and experimental models. The use of qualitative methods serve to provide deeper understanding of the results ascertained through quasi-experimental and experimental methods. Policy makers who have supported or possibly intend to support PDS programs expect hard, numeric results, signifying the effect of PDS program on student achievement.

Under the influences of *No Child Left Behind* expectations for all children in educational settings, the at standard stage suggests a commitment to provide carefully prepared research that answers the hard questions of cause and effect. Positive outcomes range from gains in test scores to gains in retention of PDS graduates as teachers in the field to gains in mentorship skills. The depth and breadth of the language in this developmental stage renders great potential for extensive research. PDS researchers, bound by the commitment to sustain the program for the benefit of students and future teachers and steeped in the support of the collaborative, have the potential to answer the call for research that measures the cause and effect of student achievement as a result of PDS. It is the mandate of the at standard stage.

LEADING STAGE

The leading stage requires advanced PDS work that is sustaining and generative, leading to systematic changes in policy and practice in partner institutions as well as impact on policy at the district, state, and national levels. At this stage of development, the PDS partnership has reached its potential for leveraging change outside its boundaries and its supporting institutions and has an impact in the broader education community. This high functioning PDS program serves as a catalyst for other programs on higher levels of policy at the district, state, and national levels. Stakeholders, well supported by the institutions, provide others with insights regarding the earlier stages of development of new and renewing PDS programs.

Due to the far reaching aspect required of this level of development, research implications suggest less control over variability than at the previous level, due to the immensity of the expectations to foster policy changes in broader educational settings. The study of regional and national changes in programs outside the original PDS setting leads to broader research methods and include: case study, survey, historical, and philosophic. These original four represent the PDS's regenerating itself in new settings, essentially creating a beginning or initial formation. When a program is developing at a distance from the original, other forms of research, including ethnography and the experimental designs, fall short because of the need for collaboration and trust to obtain personal and sensitive data, unattainable from the vantage point of expanding PDS beyond the borders of the original program. The Leading PDS serves as a promoter, compiler, and communicator of PDS research on behalf of PDS programs at all other levels, since its findings guide policy change.

REFERENCES

Barone, T., and E. Eisner. "Arts-Based Educational Research." In *Contemporary Methods for Research in Education*, edited by R. Jaeger. Washington, DC: American Education Research Association, 1998.

Campbell, D.T., and J. C. Stanley. *Experimental and Quasi-Experimental Designs for Research*. Chicago, Ill: Rand-McNally, 1963.

Greene, Maxine. "A Philosopher Looks at Qualitative Research." In *Contemporary Methods for Research in Education*, edited by R. Jaeger. Washington, DC: American Education Research Association, 1998.

Jaeger, R. *Complementary Methods for Research in Education, 2nd Edition*. Washington, D.C.: American Education Research Association, 1997.

Jaeger, R., ed. *Contemporary Methods for Research in Education*. Washington, DC: American Education Research Association, 1988.

National Council for Accreditation of Teacher Education. *Standards for Professional Development Schools*. Washington, DC: Author, 2001.

"No Child Left Behind." edited by Department of Education: United States Department of Education, 2001.

Chapter Six

PDS Research at the Beginning Stage

The NCATE PDS Standards provide a tool for PDS program personnel to assess and evaluate developmental levels of PDS program performance. Developmental Guidelines within the standards provide PDS collaborators with rubrics for determining stages of development across five standards. Through the 22 components, within the five standards, opportunities for conducting research at each developmental stage abound. Several of the components specifically address inquiry and data collection. In Chapters Six to Nine in this book, the authors consider each level of PDS program development, as delineated in the NCATE PDS Standards, and align each level with AERA recommended research practices. This chapter specifically addresses the first level in the standards labeled as *beginning stage*.

The language employed to describe the 22 elements affiliated with the beginning stage reveal several strong trends about the nature of beginning partnerships. The language describes a group of constituents who are forming their collaborative through planning and exploration and are expressing their mission and vision. *Planning and developing* constitute the majority of the descriptors. *Articulation and expression*, although prominent, have less emphasis. Other action-oriented wording include *examining and exploring*. Overall, the operative verbs in this standard support the designation of the beginning stage as a formative stage, suggesting a time when the PDS program under review is forming its partners into a collaborative.

In essence, the beginning stage of PDS program implementation involves *planning, articulating, exploring, and envisioning*. Specifically, the beginning stage description states that, "Beliefs, verbal commitments, plans, organization and initial work are consistent with the mission of PDS partnerships. This means that even at the earliest stage of development PDS partners are committed to the key concepts of PDSs and their earliest work addresses how to take initial steps in that direction." The verbs *planning, articulating, exploring, and envisioning* imply establishing or the process of establishing a PDS program. Partners at this developmental stage begin to create meaning for themselves and for future involvement by other constituents. Fundamentally, a foundation, built on shared vision and mission, sets the stage for planning and exploring the potential for the PDS program. This understanding channels research initiatives.

Within the beginning stage, references to inquiry indicate foundational establishment of the program. *Standard I: Learning Community*, parethentically states that,

> Their plans include the creation of field experiences . . . and an inquiry orientation to improve P-12 student learning, articulate a shared goal of improving and assessing the learning of P-12 students, candidates, faculty, and other professionals, express the belief that action research and other forms of inquiry are valuable tools for improving instruction, partners envision the PDS . . . exemplars of inquiry-based practice and to impel policy changes, there is a plan for creating a forum to share practices and policies (p. 17).

Standard II: Accountability, provides program participants with different perspectives of inquiry, suggesting that PDS programs

> . . . have a plan in place for the collaborative development and prioritization of important questions . . . standards for assessing all P-12 students, candidates, faculty, and other professionals' learning, explore ways to collect and report evidence . . . , collect some data about P-12 student achievement and examine the impact of current practices and norms on student learning . . . (p. 20)

Within *Standard IV: Diversity and Equity*, participating PDS partners,

> examine the gaps in achievement among racial groups . . . , examine the curricula of the university and school programs in light of issues of equity and access to knowledge by diverse learners . . . , examine multiple and varied assessment approaches to measure learning in the PDS . . . (p. 25–27)

The verbs used to describe the inquiry recommendations of *planning, articulating, and exploring* suggest foundational study of the program, thus implying foundational research approaches.

TEAM DEVELOPMENT—FORMING

The beginning level PDS, finds the constituent groups forming themselves into an entity. As the beginning level PDS forms, zeal and anxiety character-

ize the teaming effort. The many levels of understanding about teacher preparation, coupled with the needs of each group, and a desire to form a PDS, contribute to the excitement and confusion that results in a multi-directional team
situation as the group forms. A leader in the group recognizes the pattern and
provides direction. This direction, best developed through research, guides
the beginning level PDS toward cohesion, maintaining enthusiasm and mini-
mizing apprehension.

DIMENSIONS OF RESEARCH

Shulman outlines five dimensions of analysis that define a research agenda: *research problems, research settings, research investigators, research methods,
and research purposes*. Initially, research examines the problems, topics, and issues of the phenomenon under study. The first dimension, *research problems*
related to the beginning stage of PDS functioning, focuses on determining
whether the PDS partners have accomplished the establishment of a functioning partnership through shared vision and mission. Several topics emerge as research in the beginning PDS, such as plans for shared governance, diversity issues, assessment of learning, planning strategies, etc., all of which are derived
from the language of the standard. Within the context of the beginning PDS
program, the issues relate to the study of the formation of the PDS.

The *research setting,* the second dimension for studying PDS programs, di-
rects researchers to the field, which includes both the university setting and
the elementary, middle, and high schools. This setting, inherent to the phenomenon of PDS, precludes isolating classrooms, teachers, students, or candidates into artificial, lab-like settings. Particularly at the beginning stage, a
composite picture of interactions among the stakeholders, supports an authentic research setting.

When considering who should conduct research, the third dimension according to Shulman, training and background of *investigators,* becomes a
paramount issue. Generally in beginning PDS programs, in the formation
stages of the collaborative, the university contact generally emerges as investigator. Most universities require faculty maintain an active research agenda.
University personnel involved in PDS work provide the initial outlet for research in the PDS. At this early stage of PDS, some expertise in social investigation methods of research, other than experimental methods, best support
research of the beginning stage PDS. Shulman points out that, increasingly,
university personnel are coupling with classroom teachers to conduct action
research and other forms of shared investigations, within the context of
school life. This trend bears out in research of beginning PDS programs .

The term *beginning PDS* suggests initiation and early years of operation. However, as noted in Chapter Three, a PDS might operate in the beginning stage for several to many years. Consequently, in earlier years at this stage, teachers and university personnel spend time forming the team, whereas in later years at this stage, teachers' comfort level and expertise, in combination with careful guidance by university personnel, leads to shared research. As suggested in the NCATE Standards, at the beginning stage agreements brokered regarding research include action research, which takes place in classrooms, both in the university and the schools. This form of research definitely requires a shared vision and mission of the PDS. The development of the trust required to conduct research that occurs in classrooms, takes time, energy, fortitude, and finesse.

Research *methods,* the fourth dimension employed in educational settings as articulated by Shulman, extend beyond the earlier, isolated forms of experimental and quasi-experimental. Contributions from anthropology, sociology, linguistics, socio-linguistics, and other humanist fields provide a wealth of approaches that authenticate a lived phenomenon such as PDS. These qualitative methods add to the richness of the quantitative. Among the eight methods outlined: arts-based, historical, philosophic, ethnographic, case study, survey, comparative experimental, and quasi-experimental, several emerge as especially suitable to the beginning stage. However, this does not preclude the application of the other methods in the study of the beginning PDS. The methods recommended here show specific potential for capturing the essence of the beginning developmental stage as articulated in the description of the standard. Therefore, case study, survey, ethnographic, and historical methods are recommended for studying the beginning stage of PDS operation. These four methods require field studies to ascertain the inner workings of the setting, which at this stage of PDS development appears imperative due to the foundational functioning of the program. Each method is detailed later in this chapter, referring specifically to the beginning stage of PDS development.

The fifth dimension of research, *purpose*, refers to reasons for conducting the research. Shulman suggests that researchers' purposes vary across a gamut of possibilities. These could include the development of a theory, development of new strategies to solve a problem, create a more complete description of a situation, improve policy, connect theory to practice, extend theory, formulation of general principles, and many more. Multiple purposes transpire when considering the beginning stage of PDS. Among these, to create a more complete description of the PDS program, aligns with the tenets of this stage of PDS functioning. In order to better understand how collaborators are *planning, articulating, exploring, and envisioning* the PDS, the research purpose of creating a more complete description seems apt. An examination of published research in PDS provides numerous studies that describe PDS programs at the beginning stage. The reader should note that the studies described in this chapter are hypothetical illustrations and represent research protocol as recommended in the AERA contemporary research methods.

MATCHED METHODS OF AERA RESEARCH AND NCATE BEGINNING STAGE

Case Study

As discussed in Chapter Five, case study, a sociological method, focuses on the study of one situation, in this case, a single PDS program, in the forming stages of collaborative development. The issues at the formative stage of collaborative development concentrate on knowing the levels of agreement and understanding among stakeholders. Blanchard describes the forming stage of collaborative development as one with high motivation and commitment and low organizational qualities. The issue at this stage becomes one of focus on the dynamics of constituents toward a common understanding of the PDS program as a shared enterprise between schools and the university. The setting for this study is the beginning stage PDS. Depending on the point in the life of the beginning PDS, the investigators could vary. A PDS in its very early inception, less than one year, will most likely require skills and expertise of university researchers. However, when the PDS has been in operation for several years at the beginning stage, it is common for new investigators, such as teachers and school administrators, to enter the realm of investigator. The purpose of the case study is to determine the level of understanding of all constituents of the newly formed PDS and cohesiveness that results from agreements across disparate groups contributing to the process of forming the program.

Data sources that aid in the study of the formative PDS case can include, but are not exclusive to: observation notes, school and university documents, test scores, conversation notes, university curriculum, placement schedules, minutes from meetings, surveys, agreement documents, and many more. In essence, the researcher attempts to define the what, where, how, when, and why of how the newly forming PDS is functioning within the context of *planning, articulating, exploring, and envisioning* the PDS. In a beginning PDS, collaborators work to define the vision, mission, research agendas, components of diversity, shared approaches to intertwining of university and schools toward the common good of P-12 learners and the collaborative. A case study approach provides a mechanism for researching these phenomena at this stage of development.

A Sample Case Study

A PDS program that had been in existence for several years collapsed under state certification changes and was forced to undergo complete reconstruction. The newly constructed PDS sought the assistance of a university
researcher/instructor, also known as the site coordinator, to initiate the reconstructive process. To that end, the coordinator elicited the assistance of
principals, district personnel, university supervisors, and teachers to form a new
PDS program. The problem under investigation was team/collaborative development. The questions focused on what it took on the part of the different constituents to initiate and sustain a newly formed PDS striving toward collaboration as a team, how the different constituents came together to form the
collaborative team, and who made which contributions to the process of forming the collaborative. The setting was a rural/urban school district that had previously engaged in PDS practice with three separate cadres of teacher candidates
and involving nine schools. Multiple data sources including minutes from initial
meetings, surveys of all constituents, including PDS candidates, anecdotal
records of conversations, agreement documents, mentor teacher development
training agendas, and candidate emails served as data sources. The site coordinator served as the initial investigator in the case study. By the second year of
the newly formed program, several teachers, in conjunction with the site coordinator, initiated studies particular to the interests of the teachers.

   In keeping with the tenets of the beginning stage of PDS, the case study
sought to render an image of a PDS as it *planned, articulated, explored, and
envisioned* itself in the newly formed configuration. Initially, the site coordinator met with potential principals to ascertain their prior experiences and interest in constructing a new form of PDS program. Among the twelve interviewed, nine principals showed interest. The principals met with the site
coordinator and created mission and vision statements dealing with the infu-
sion of candidates into the regular school program and the needs and expectations of the candidates and teachers. Annual surveys of teachers, principals,
candidates, and supervisors, based on high performance team components of
purpose, empowerment, relationships/communication, flexibility, optimal
performance, recognition, and morale had suggested in the earlier years of the
PDS initiative that teachers and candidates' perception of empowerment
waned in comparison to that of the principals. In the second and third years,
teachers empowered to create rotation schedules for interns during the first
semester, became more invested in the process of developing the collaborative. The development and increased membership among teachers on a field-
based research team led to further study of teacher teaming across schools. Interns empowered to create the content and context for weekly seminars in the

second semester, increased their investment in the collaborative development. Emails and conversations with interns suggested recognition on the part of the candidate as a constituent in the process of developing the PDS program, rather than a receiver of PDS programming on the part of the university and schools.

As seen in the above illustration, the case study, incorporating multiple documents and forms of data collecting, depicts a PDS program in the reconstructive process as it contemplates its existence and the future of its continuation. As the case study continues, consequently, the additional items listed in the beginning stage: student test scores, study of resource allocation, skills and knowledge of faculty, and forms of recognition, can fold into the ongoing investigation of the collaboration's development. This example demonstrates the validity of case study use as a viable form of studying the beginning stage of PDS program development.

Survey

Survey research, while possibly a component of case study, also stands alone as a method of research. According to Jaeger, survey research seeks to describe "specific characteristics of a large group or persons, objects, or institutions" (p. 449). Jaegar suggests that survey research involves three components: (1) specific facts, (2) well-defined groups, and (3) knowledge of the present condition of the group under investigation. Population, population parameter, sample, and representative sample, important components of survey research, direct the researcher to seek groups that clearly represent the condition of the group and/or institution, in its current circumstance. Typically, surveys involve paper and pencil bubbling of responses to stems or questions eliciting specific facts about or attitudes toward the current condition of the situation surveyed. A second form of survey, interview protocol, elicits similar information, with the additional benefit of unsolicited responses, providing possibly more depth, personal perception, and supplementary information that provide greater elucidation of the situation under study. As a rule, this form of survey requires face-to-face contact, or at the least, video to video. With the advent of emails, surveys, through either chat rooms and discussion boards, the potential for increasing survey data among people involved in PDS programs through strategic questioning increases immeasurably.

A Sample Survey Study

A teacher research team was formed during the second year of the reconstructed PDS program for the purpose of engaging teachers in the inquiry process. In the first year of the reconstruction, teachers, empowered to create placement schedules for the semester of observation, created rotation schedules that introduced the interns to all the mentor teachers as well as all other aspects of the building, including cafeteria, custodian, librarian, office staff, cafeteria, Special Education, Art, and Physical Education. Teachers, encouraged to study issues germane to their role as mentor, posed a problem regarding intern placement in the observation semester of the PDS year. They questioned the value of differing placement schema toward the understanding of schooling, by the interns, from a teaching perspective. The teachers, with the guidance and support of the university site coordinator, created a survey to ascertain the interns,' teachers,' and principals' perceptions of the interns' understanding of schooling based on their experiences in the rotation schemes.

The PDS program used between eight and ten elementary schools for intern placements. There were four placements, two in each of two consecutive semesters. In the first semester each intern spent seven weeks, two full days a week, in each of two schools, constituting the first two placements. The purpose of two school placements served to introduce the interns to the district's highly divergent populations. No fewer than three and no more than four interns were placed in any school. Each school offered two mentors for each intern, between six and eight mentors. The interns, during the first semester of two, spent time learning about schooling from the perspective of a professional rather than a student. To circulate students through the school(s) to learn about the varying programs, teachers from each school, during a mentor in-service meeting, created schedules employing the following limitations: 14 seven-hour days into which must be scheduled (1) time with each of six/eight mentors, (2) time with the ancillary school personnel, and (3) time in other instructional areas. Each school team created schedules that suited their view of the limitations.

In the first year, the schemes for rotation varied considerably. Several teams had interns spending time with only three of the six teachers based on prior experience. Several teams relinquished their responsibility to assistant principals. Several teams created schedules that limited the amount of time interns spent with mentors and increased time they spent in areas outside the classroom. One team directed interns to spend half days with each mentor, completing a treasure hunt in the school, finding each of the non-classroom aspects of the school on their own.

At the end of the semester, the teacher team conducted a survey of interns, teachers, and principals, regarding the effectiveness of the rotation schedules on intern understanding of schooling. The survey included three lines of questioning: (1) Who designed the survey and where was the schedule implemented? (2) How was the rotation designed? and (3) What effect did the rotation have on intern understanding of schooling, from a professional perspective? The survey was issued by the university site coordinator to the principals and interns during end of the semester meetings. The mentor teachers from the research team collected data from other mentor teachers. The findings revealed several interesting trends: whoever created the schedule deemed it effective in informing interns about schooling as professionals. In essence, if principals created the schedule, they saw it as positive, whereas mentor teachers, under the instruction of assistant principals who took over the scheduling, found the same schedule less effective. Likewise, teachers who created their own schedule generally saw the schedule as effective, with the exception of those who scheduled interns to rotate twice daily and/or engaged the interns in extensive time away from the classroom. The findings informed the teacher research team as to how to support its fellow teachers in creating more efficient, teacher directed schedules for the next year. Data from the study, presented at a principal meeting, encouraged all principals and assistants to release the responsibility for scheduling to the mentor teachers.

This hypothetical survey research demonstrates the tenets of the beginning state of the NCATE PDS Standards for *planning, articulating, exploring, and envisioning*. The PDS program, by conducting survey research within the context of its early development, shows how plans are being laid to "include the creation of field experiences and clinical practice to provide candidates with opportunities for full immersion in the learning community" (p. 21). The teacher research team, in conjunction with the university site coordinator, envisioned teachers as empowered to contribute to the process of PDS programming that addressed the issue of immersion in the learning community. The survey study, though simple, was used to explore the planning of mentor teachers and serves as an example of survey research at the beginning stage of the NCATE Standards.

Historical Research

Historical research, an inductive process, leads researchers to gather information and infer about the circumstance under the investigation. The information gathered includes facts, figures, and specific details that occurred in a particular period in time, albeit a short or long period. Kaestle considers historical research part science and part art. The science, the details gathered in the inquiry, and the art, the crafting of interpretation of the historical event. Through the inductive process of gathering, chronicling, sorting, and inferring, historical inquiry provides a defined picture of a period of time, an event, or a set of historical circumstances. In the beginning stage of the PDS, history encompasses the life of the PDS program, a series of teacher-training sessions or a cycle of meetings that resulted in the development of mission and vision statements. No matter the historical inquiry conducted in the PDS, facts, figures, and specific detail always help to inform the partnership's development.

Incorporation of theory when conducting historical inquiry aids in different ways. Theory guides evidence gathering in addition to what is acceptable as evidence. Theory also guides in the development of arguments when inferences are made regarding evidence gathered. In 1986 The Holmes Group developed the theory of professional development schools, based on evidence from *A Nation at Risk*, that implied a need for school reform. The Holmes Group theorized that if teachers received preparation employing the medical model of internship and residency, nurtured by a clinical staff (teachers) and instructed in the resident placement (schools), their knowledge and skills as teachers would vastly improve, rendering learning in settings taught under teachers prepared in this manner, of higher caliber. Historical research in PDS provides a clear picture of the development of PDS as a phenomenon in the United States and the application of those principles.

A Sample Historical Study

As the PDS program continued to develop, it reached the point where it included more PDS sites than could be managed by the original faculty who had started the program. Growth in candidate enrollment, mandates from the state to employ PDS as the means for preparing all initial certification teachers, and geographic expansion of PDS sites farther from the university, forced the program leadership to include unprepared personnel in the process of overseeing PDS programs. The problem of increasing the number of PDS sites, consequently, coordinators, resulted in a lack of historical reference to the program. The questions of who, why, where, when, and what remained open-ended.

To more clearly comprehend the history of the PDS' previous operations, a newly appointed PDS site coordinator embarked on an oral history study of the PDS program. Reading many of the original Holmes documents led the researcher to theorize that a shared collaborative approach to the mechanization of PDS requires careful inquiry of standing programs prior to embarking on further development. To that end, the researcher posed several questions: (1) How did the program begin? (2) Who was instrumental in initiating and maintaining the program? (3) What motivated the development of the PDS at the university? (4) How did university and school personnel collaborate/co-operate to create the program, and (5) Where was the program in its development at the time of the study?

The researcher spent three years collecting oral history data. The data sources, original PDS coordinators (university personnel), principals, teachers, and interns, provided facts, figures, and specific detail about the history of the PDS as they knew it. Contributors, when asked to describe their knowledge and experience in PDS, provided taped interviews and/or email responses to open-ended questions. The interviews, conducted in an emic style, allowed participants the freedom, during 30–45 minutes, to describe their personal experience and recollection of PDS. In an emic style interview there are no questioning strategies, protocols, or pre-formed notions of the direction of the interview. The interviewer poses a point of discussion concerning the area of study and interviewees lead the response, based on their perspective of the circumstance under study. The transcribed data revealed over 80 percent of the conversation occurred among respondents, rather than by the researcher, suggesting a wealth of information from respondents.

Transcripts of the tapes, incorporated into an electronic data analysis program, provided the researcher with the possibility to analyze the responses for trends and patterns in the understanding by the professors, principals, teachers, and interns of the PDS during that time. A grounded approach to data analysis, whereby the researcher reads each statement of each respondent and codes the responses into emergent categories, served to create the initial focus of analysis. Each category, further analyzed, provided deeper understanding of the PDS program during that time. A third analysis, conducted within pre-developed categories for the study of leadership in the PDS, provided another means by which to examine the history of the program.

Findings from this historical study suggested a strong agreement among interviewees. All university personnel provided the same story of a new idea for teacher preparation placed on them by the state through a grant. Some of the initial professors, principals, and teachers benefited from the grant with visits to programs in other parts of the United States. In addition, they applied grant money to initiate technological connections between the schools and the university. The program began with courses taught on elementary and middle school campuses and engaged two schools and six professors. Professors worked toward building cooperative agreements between school personnel and the university.

Eventually, due to the burgeoning population of students who enrolled in the program, instruction returned to the university campus. Several things happened when the program shifted control to the university rather than the shared governance. University faculty reported greater strains on relationships with school personnel due to their limited presence in the schools. This finding was supported by the comments among school personnel. The reaction from school personnel ranged from deep concern to complete acceptance. Some schools, relieved to have their space returned, accepted the change in the program and continued to support PDS intern placements. However, other schools chose to abandon the program, citing lack of communication and collaboration.

Interns interviewed indicated variability of perspective of the program. Many noted the lack of communication between the schools and university, citing several incidents of not knowing their university PDS site coordinator. A general trend of interns as receivers of PDS programming, rather than contributors to the process, suggested alienation from the intent of PDS, to create a sense of community between interns, university faculty, and school personnel. However, in many cases interns reported the excellence of their preparation as teachers, based on the theory-to-practice approach taken in the university classes, as the coursework tied to field placements.

These findings informed the PDS researcher and helped guide the reconstruction of the older PDS program in one district. This historical research in a beginning stage PDS program provided impetus for shared conversations, guided the site coordinator, and propelled the PDS program toward development of a collaborative through *planning, articulating, exploring, and envisioning* the potential for the PDS program. Oral history aligns with the NCATE PDS Standards at the beginning stage due to its probing nature to determine the perception of the constituency of leadership in the program as it is forming itself into a collaborative, working team.

SUPPORT FOR RESEARCH AT THE BEGINNING STAGE

What makes research happen at the beginning stage includes tenacity, persistence, simplicity, vision, research skills, and teaming. Researchers of early PDS programs, generally university personnel, often get caught up in the business of maintaining relationships among constituents, such as teaching classes, conducting meetings, and the like. Creating research agendas that meet standards of excellence, while serving as participant observers, produces challenges. Keeping the research simple aids in the process of conducting it at this level. Studying the *planning, articulating, exploring, and envisioning* process, outlined in the NCATE PDS Standards, provides a catalyst for research problems, questions, settings, and data sources. Knowing and using the research skills, aids in decisions regarding what kind of research to conduct. Teaming with other faculty, graduate students, teachers, and other district personnel fosters support for research agendas. However, time spent training others in research methodology and data collection often requires much more investment than if the research were conducted alone. Consequently, simple, focused research agendas based on the study of a forming team, can serve to guide research decisions at the beginning stage.

To perform research well, resources in the form of financial support, course release, and graduate student assistance, can liberate researchers. Financial support, in the form of grants, endowments, program budget, state, district, and/or university commitments, can provide researchers with wherewithal to study program development. Time, a valuable and necessary component required to conduct excellent research in the field, is best supported with course release or graduate assistants. These two tools provide researchers with the necessary time to both develop grant proposals and maintain them, when awarded, with assistance. The researcher in the beginning PDS program, crucial to the continued development of the PDS program through developing, at standard, and leading levels, requires tenaciousness and resilience.

REFERENCES

Abma, Sherry, John Fischetti, and Ann Larson. "The Purpose of a Professional Development School Is to Make a Difference: 10 Years of a High." *Peabody Journal of Education* 74, no. 5 (1999): 254–58.

Birrell, James R., James R. Young, M. Winston Egan, Margaret R. Ostlund, Paul F. Cook, Cathy B. Tibbitts, and Paul F. DeWitt. "Deinstitutionalizing Teacher Preparation in a Collaborative, School-Based Program." *Professional Educator* 20, no. 3 (1998): 25–36.

Blanchard, K., P. Zigarmi, and D Zigarmi. *Leadership and the One Minute Manager-Increasing Effectiveness through Situational Leadership.* New York William Morrow and Company, 1985.

Blanchard, Ken, Patricia Zigarmi, and Drea Zigarmi. *Leadership and the One Minute Manager—Increasing Effectivensss through Situational Leadership.* New York: William Morrow and Company, 1985.

Bondy, Elizabeth. "A Partnership of Projects: Becoming an Elementary Professional Development School." *Peabody Journal of Education* 74, no. 3/4 (1999): 42–58.

Campoy, Renee. "Professional Development Schools Can Revitalize Teacher Education." *USA Today Magazine*, may 1997 1997, 68–70.

Clark, Richard J., and Donna E. LaLonde. "A Case for Department-Based Professional Development Sites for Secondary Teacher Education." *Journal of teacher education* 43, no. 1 (1992): 35–41.

Cuban, Larry. "The Holmes Group Report: Why Reach Exceeds Grasp." *Teachers College Record* 88, no. 3 (1987): 48–53.

Darling-Hammond, Linda. "Schools for Tomorrow's Teachers." *Teachers college record* 88, no. 3 (1987): 354–58.

Dee, Jay, Alan Henkin, and Sally Pell. "Support for Innovation in Stie-Based-Management Schools: Developing a Climate for Change." *Educational research quarterly* 25, no. 4 (2002): 36–50.

DeWitt, Paul F., James R. Birrell, M. Winston Egan, Paul F. Cook, Margaret F. Ostlund, and James R. Young. "Professional Development Schools and Teacher Educators' Beliefs: Challenges and Change." *Teacher Education Quarterly* 25, no. 2 (1998): 63–80.

Education, United States National Commission on Excellence in. "A Nation at Risk: The Imperative for Educational Reform." 65. Washington, D.C.: United States Department of Education: National Commission ofr Excellence in Education, 1983.

Freese, Anne R. "Professional Development School." *Teaching and teacher education* 15, no. 8 (1999): 895–909.

Fullan, Michael. "The School as a Learning Organization: Distant Dreams." *Theory into practice* 34, no. 4 (1995): 230–36.

Gebhard, Meg. "A Case for Professional Development Schools." *TESOL Quarterly* 32, no. 3 (1998): 501–10.

Jaeger, R. *Complementary Methods for Research in Education, 2nd Edition*. Washington, D.C.: American Education Research Association, 1997.

Jaeger, Richard. "Survey Methods in Educational Research." In *Complementary Methods for Research in Education*, edited by Richard Jaeger. Washington, D.C.: American Educational Research Association, 1997.

Kaestle, Carl. "Historical Methods in Educational Research." In *Contemporary Methods for Research in Education; 2nd Edition*, edited by Richard Jaeger. Washington, D.C.: American Educational Research Association, 1997.

Koerner, Marti. "The Cooperating Teacher: An Ambivalent Participant in Student Teaching." *Journal of teacher education* 43, no. 1 (1992): 46–56.

Kyle, Diane W., Gayle H. Moore, and Judy L Sanders. "The Role of the Mentor Teacher: Insights, Challenges, and Implications." *Peabody Journal of Education* 74, no. 5 (1999): 109–23.

Lecos, Mary Anne, Carol Cassella, Cynthia Evans, Cathy Leahy, Enid Liess, and Tina Lucas. "Empowering Teacher Leadership in Professional Development Schools." *Teaching & Change* 8, no. 1 (2000): 98–114.

Levine, Marsha. "Standards for Professional Development Schools." 34. Alexandria, Virginia: national council for accreditation of teacher education, 2001.

Mayes, Clifford. "The Holmes Report: Perils and Possibilities." *Teaching and Teacher Education* 14, no. 8 (1998): 775–92.

Nelson, Mark D. "Professional Development Schools: An Implementation Model." *NASSP Bulletin* 82, no. 600 (1998): 93–103.

Patterson, J. L. *Leadership for Tomorrow's Schools*. Alexandria, VA: Association for Supervision adn Curriculum Development, 1993.

Sargent, Barbara. "Finding Good Teachers and Keeping Them." *Educational Leadership* 60, no. 8 (2003): 44–48.

Schletchty, P.C. *Schools for the 21st Century: Leaderhsip Imperatives for Educaitonal Reform*. San Francisco: CA: Jossey-Bass, 1990.

Shulman, Lee. "The Nature of Disciplined Inquiry in Education." In *Contemporary Methods for Research in Education, 2nd Edition*, edited by Richard Jaeger. Washington, D.C.: American Education Research Association, 1997.

"Standards for Professional Development Schools." Washington, D.C.: National Council for Accreditation of Teacher Education, 2001.

Stroble, Beth, and Henry Luka. "It's My Life, Now: The Impact of Professional Development School Partnerships on University and School Administrators." *Peabody journal of education* 74, no. 5 (1999): 123–36.

Teitel, Lee. "Looking toward the Future by Understanding the Past: The Historical Context of Professional." *Peabody Journal of Education* 74, no. 3/4 (1999): 6–21.

——. "Separations, Divorces, and Open Marriages in Professional Development School Partnerships." *Journal of teacher education* 49, no. 2 (1998): 85–96.

Walters, Susan, and Flynn Pritchard. "The Complexity of Partnering: A Case Study of Two Middle School Professional Development Schools." *Peabody Journal of Education* 74, no. 5 (1999): 58–65.

Wise, Authur E., and Marsha Levine. "The 10-Step Solution." *Education Week* 21, no. 24 (2002): 56–58.

Chapter Seven

PDS Research at the Developing Stage

An analysis of the operative verbs in the description of the developing stage of the standards point to two strong issues: (1) data-driven decision making and (2) shared responsibility. Across the 22 elements, each issue received notice no fewer than ten times. These two issues characterize this level of PDS development. The added expectation for partners to find common ground, with levels of shared responsibility, to forward the understanding of the effect of PDS on student learning through research and data collection among all constituents, entails extensive interaction and high levels of trust.

The first, data-driven decision making, suggests a need to collect data, analyze it, and use the information to make decisions. To achieve any of these steps requires collaboration, rather than cooperation. Collaboration, "the act of working together for a common goal," differs from cooperation, "doing what is asked or required." The former suggests shared responsibility in decision making, whereas the latter advocates an autocratic system of leadership and following. At the developing stage, all constituents contribute and participate in the process of gathering data, analyzing it, and deciding as a collective the meaning of the data and the effect of that meaning on decision making. The importance of the collaborative becomes essential, particularly regarding the collection of student achievement data. Schools, in collaboration with universities, require assurances that data collected, are used and reported under the strictest guidelines. Likewise, universities collecting data on university student performance must assure protection under Federal Educational Rights and Privacy Act (FERPA) and other federal guidelines for reporting achievement. A key issue, trust in professional treatment of data and reporting, leads the shared responsibility for data collection.

An analysis of the language of the NCATE PDS Standards at the developing stage regarding the first issue, research and data-driven decision making, suggests different constituents may be operating at different levels of commitment and understanding. In Standard I, the following language supports this position.

Inquiry and action research are being used in some classrooms, but there may not be a clear conception of connections among the learning of P-12 students, candidates, and experienced educators. Some university and school faculty visit classrooms to observe each other's practice and to collect and share data; some use student outcome data to modify curriculum and instruction.

Further support found in Standard II systematically outlines the flow of data collection, processing, and reporting:

> PDS partners develop several important questions related to P-12 student, candidate, faculty, and other professionals' learning. Data are collected systematically to answer questions. Partners analyze data together and make some changes in practice as a result. . . format for reporting evidence about faculty knowledge, skills, and dispositions is in place. . . PDS partners underscore their commitment to making informed choices . . . PDS partners collect data from multiple sources and examine them systematically to identify the impact of individual teaching practices on P-12 student achievement.

Standard IV suggests an additional form of research, noted in this quote from the standards, "PDS partners conduct some research to assess effectiveness of the PDS partnership, and to evaluate future needs." The implication in the developing stage of PDS, regarding research in the PDS, that partners work together to find ways to research both student success on standardized measures, but also, the functioning of the PDS, implies that PDS constituents share responsibility.

Standard V recommends "PDS partners conduct some research to assess effectiveness of the PDS partnership, and to evaluate future needs." This recommendation, by the use of the word "effect," suggests quasi-experimental and/or experimental designs. Both of these designs direct researchers to separate groups, either through volunteerism (quasi) or through random selection (experimental). Facilitation of these research designs requires a firm establishment of trust, shared responsibility, and the commitment to the collection and use of data for decision making. In the climate of high-stakes testing, the willingness to trust that randomly selecting groups into experimental and control treatments will not impede student success on standardized measures, challenges the best of relationships between schools and universities.

The second issue inherent in the language of the standard, shared responsibility essential to the cohesion of well-formed collaborative groups, requires high levels of trust, continuous communication, and deep understanding by constituents of the circumstances of each others' situation. This perspective of the members of the PDS team suggests a group of disparate contributors who recognize differences in leadership, expectations for PDS work in their setting, and the demands the PDS process places on each contributing member of the team. Shared responsibility necessitates compromise and consensus, hence the need for continuous communication. Trust and openness provide the basis for success in achieving the essence of shared responsibility.

Standard I provides the language of expectation for all constituents, including candidates, school personnel, and university personnel: "Candidates share responsibility with PDS partners for the learning of P-12 students. University faculty share their expertise, skills, and knowledge to support school improvement and candidate learning." In this same standard, more expectations for shared responsibility take the form of shared governance and policy development, "PDS partners are represented on each other's governing and policy boards. PDS partnership has developed a forum for sharing practices and policies across PDSs and affiliated schools." These three expectations set forth in this standard provide a clear path of shared responsibility from student achievement, to participating with each other on related policy-making bodies, to forums for reporting the results of collaborative work.

Standard II sets additional expectations for shared responsibility with the implication that all constituents accept responsibility for members' growth outside the group members' home operation. "Candidate assessment is seen as a shared responsibility among partners, with a greater range of assessments in place or being planned." The implication, that potentially all constituents, not just university personnel, take responsibility for assessing candidate success, requires a higher level of responsibility, in addition to higher levels of trust among constituents. An additional implication, that university personnel trust school and district personnel to assess candidate progress and excellence, points to shared responsibility.

Standard III refers to shared responsibilities with regard to difficult issues, such as resources and beliefs. "There is evidence of parity in some of the decision making processes and resource allocations. PDS partner institutions respect and value the beliefs, needs, and goals of all participants. Partners depend on each other to accomplish some of their professional goals." The interdependency indicated creates an image of constituents who not only know each other's beliefs, needs, and goals, but also work toward communal ways to go about achieving these. This points to the need for continuous communication and high levels of trust. School personnel, under pressure to perform to state and national standards, and university personnel under pressure to produce research on their involvement in PDS, create a natural alienation from each other's needs. However, through careful communication and support, both can support each other's needs, goals, and beliefs. The achievement of shared responsibility lays the groundwork for potential research on a deeper level, research that provides focus for decision-making and program improvement.

TEAM DEVELOPMENT—STORMING

As the team of developing PDS continues to form itself, with higher levels of trust, shared responsibility, and deeper investigation into the workings and effectiveness of the program, the likelihood of discontent grows. The storming level of team formation correlates with the developing stage of the NCATE PDS standards. During the storming level, team members offer their perspective, defend it, and struggle with contributions and needs of others. In the PDS, the site coordinator from the university might see the PDS as a research agenda, leading to publications and eventually tenure, but not recognize the limitations of the principals and teachers in the schools. Likewise, the school leadership might expect interns from the university to participate in school activities that interfere with university expectations. These differences in perspective create the perfect storm. To facilitate research in a storming atmosphere requires a coaching leadership style to guide the team through the discrepancies and discordances. A transformative style of leadership carries the collaborative group through the situational moments of keeping the group together, while getting the research done.

DIMENSIONS OF RESEARCH

Research dimensions at this level change, increase in rigor, and in possibilities due to the shared responsibility of the partnership members. *Research problems* reflect concerns about student achievement and success of the program as a tool to reach all constituents. The developing stage *setting*, wrought with both potential and conflict, provides a rich environment in which to conduct research. *Settings* at this stage include the inside of classrooms, both in the school and the university. *Research investigators*, in a well developed collaborative include mentor teachers, possibly as MAT or M.Ed. students at the university, university personnel, doctoral students serving as PDS coordinators or mentor teachers, doctoral students interested in PDS, and teacher candidates conducting action research as part of their coursework. *Research methods* possibilities increase dramatically due to the increased trust and shared responsibility. These include: quasi-experimental, historical, case study, survey, philosophical, arts-based, and ethnographic methods. The only method from the AERA list remaining outside the realm of this stage, experimental research, would be difficult to manage at this stage, due to the storming nature of the developing group. To achieve an experimental study, random groups, tested in blind studies, requires a higher level of trust and group functioning than seems possible at this stage of development. The twofold *purpose of research* at this stage, to determine the level of functioning of the PDS and effect of PDS programming on student achievement, leads researchers to multiple methods of research.

In the seven hypothetical studies described as examples of research at the developing stage, a PDS program in operation for five years serves as the research site. The program operated under the leadership of the same university coordinator, functioned within a single school district, and operated with five elementary and two middle schools for three years. Candidates participated in the year-long program as participant observers in the first semester and student teachers in the second. The candidates attended methods classes in mathematics, science, social studies, and language arts two days a week and spent two days in the field each week, observing and assisting. The number of schools involved in the program increased from 7 to 13 in the fourth year, following a doubling of the PDS program enrollment from 25 to 50. Until the fourth year of the program, candidates' main responsibility in the field consisted of assisting mentor teachers. In the fourth year, during the first semester, candidates assumed the role of tutor in addition to general observer and helper. Using the NCATE PDS Standards and self-study, the group determined after the third year that the program ranked at the developing stage. The studies described here provide a window into the research conducted by this PDS program. Each method of research applied to the program presented below, is followed by a summary of the relationship between research conducted and the two issues specific to the developing stage: research-based decision making and shared responsibility.

Quasi-experimental

In the fourth year of the program, the leadership team chose to study the effect of tutoring in mathematics on student achievement in mathematics. The problem noted, poor performance by elementary and middle school students in mathematics on state mandated examinations and pointed out by principals from the participating schools, prompted the university instructor of mathematics methods, affiliated with the PDS program, to reconstruct the math methods course to align with tutor preparation for candidates. The thirteen schools in the PDS identified students in need of tutoring, employing a general district diagnostic measure and previous years' mathematics test scores. The candidates administered an additional standardized diagnostic to determine the specific mathematics needs of each child. Following all diagnoses, six children were either randomly assigned to each candidate or intentionally assigned, based on teachers' recommendations.

Each candidate tutored six children each week, twice weekly for six weeks, then post-diagnosed all children originally tested, with the same instrument. The result of the study showed a significant difference in scores, at the .05 level, among students who received tutoring from candidates. In addition, candidates reported that their understanding of mathematics and the pedagogy related teaching mathematics increased immensely, due to the opportunities afforded in the tutoring project. Based on the results, the tutoring project became a part of the PDS program in all elementary and middle schools the following year. During the fifth year of the program, mentor teachers organized and worked with candidates to accommodate weekly tutoring interventions, employing a quasi-experimental design in over 90 percent of the schools. The mathematics instructor continued to accommodate the needs of the district with course adjustments, and interns continued to tutor six children each week for six weeks.

Historical

The PDS program initiated an historical study of the program, documenting the first three years. The purpose of the study was to determine the understanding by all constituents of the mission and vision of the program, as viewed from their historical perspective. During the three years of the program's development, candidates, mentor teachers, principals, university personnel, and district personnel met frequently, in separate constituent groups, to discuss and share ideas about the direction of the program. Minutes from over twenty meetings provided historical perspective of the various groups. In addition, emails from various members of the PDS constituency served as historical evidence of the functioning of the group.

At the end of three years, members of each constituent group met for a one-day conference to discuss, share, and create mission and vision statements for the PDS program. During the conference, members of each group convened in mixed groups to analyze the current level of development of the PDS program, based on the NCATE PDS Standards. The results of the document analysis of three years of minutes and emails, notes from the conference, and informal interviews, resulted in an understanding of the program's developmental position, a platform for decision making, and a mandate to continue to develop. The historical overview showed the program progressing from a beginning stage to developing at the third year mark. The resulting mission and vision statements embraced the notion of shared responsibility for the betterment of students, candidates, and education in general. In the fourth year, the group used the developed mission and vision statements to direct the program into more research, empowerment of teachers and candidates, and higher levels of trust among university and school leaders.

Case Study

A mentor teacher in the program, involved in the masters program at the university, initiated an action research project in the fourth year of the program. The purpose of the study, to better understand children's interpersonal intelligence, involved an investigation of children's discourse during reading/writing group time. Data sources included a daily journal, observation checklists, and a survey of student understanding of interpersonal intelligence as noted in children's literature. The data collectors included the teacher, two other mentor teachers, school administrators, PDS candidates, and a university coordinator. The researcher administered a diagnostic survey, a checklist of indicators of interpersonal intelligence, using a children's book that told the story of two friends working together toward resolution of a problem.

Candidates, other mentor teachers, and administrators observed the children during reading centers time and documented their interpersonal exchanges. Each observer used a checklist of interpersonal intelligence behaviors and language. The teacher maintained a journal of student responses to class activities that focused on interpersonal intelligence characteristics found in children's literature. The university coordinator worked with the mentor teacher to document the research. Results of the study showed that children overall showed gains in interpersonal intelligence, particularly in their ability to infer qualities associated with interpersonal intelligent, as defined by Howard Gardner. The primary learning for the teacher from the study, that interpersonal intelligence among young children through the study of the characteristics of interpersonal intelligence noted in children's literature, enhances their understanding of empathy, collaboration, and effective communication in reading centers. Subsequent to this study, the mentor teacher changed her practice in presenting children's literature, emphasizing the interpersonal intelligence aspects of the literary works. In addition, interns, employed in the district as first year teachers, used the practice of presenting children's literature from an interpersonal intelligence perspective.

Survey

The PDS program, designed on the Team Development Model, empowers constituent teams of principals, mentor teachers, candidates, and supervisors to contribute to the process of the program implementation. The purpose of the survey research, to study the disposition of team members toward the program from the perspective of their empowered role in the program, provided the program with longitudinal data on the issues of understanding, empowerment, and commitment to the program. A survey designed to ascertain the disposition of each constituent team on the seven levels of a high performing team and administered to each participating member of the PDS program, provided data on current levels of team development. Contrived from the acronym PERFORM, the survey posed stem statements for each word affiliated with the letter in the acronym. The acronym stood for: P—understands purpose; E—sense of empowerment; R—relationships and communication; F—flexibility; O—optimal performance; R—recognition, and M—morale. Each constituent group rated each aspect a high performing team from the perspective of their involvement in the program and the basis of their empowerment.

The survey, administered four consecutive years, revealed trends in increased levels of perception of empowerment and inclusion in the team. The implication, the program constituents perceived themselves as members of a high performing team. The data from the first few years guided change in procedures and support systems, netting a shift in perception from team member to team player. Results also provided guidance in changes of ways to empower candidates, generally perceived as receivers, rather than contributors in the PDS process. By the fourth year, ratings exceeded 95 percent acceptance across all constituent groups, confirming the development of the team. Each constituent group continues, in the fifth year of the program, to contribute and accept responsibilities for the functioning of the program.

Philosophical

Hermeneutics, the science and methodology of interpreting documents, a key component of philosophical research, led to the study of candidate philosophical positioning on the issue of teacher identity formation. Teacher identity formation, the development of self as teacher, occurs through the process of self-examination, critique, and reflection. The purpose of the study, conducted in the fourth year of the program, to create an understanding of how candidates perceive their identity as teachers in formation, led to the examination of multiple documents that captured the voice of candidates as they sorted through their self-examination. The documents included weekly emails during two semesters of the internship, portfolios at the end of the first and second semesters, and taped exit interviews at the end of the year.

Maslow (1962) provided a hierarchy of need, that served as a lens to analyze data. The hierarchy represents four levels of need: subsistence, belonging, esteem of others, and self-actualization. Maslow suggests that individuals continue to work toward self-actualization for their entire lives. However, recent studies of the hierarchy suggest that a level beyond self-actualization, transcendence, whereby self-actualized people reach beyond themselves to others in need, lifts a person above the original hierarchy. Maimonedes, a thirteenth century philosopher, developed a hierarchy of giving, whereby at the highest of seven levels, the contributor gives the recipient the freedom to learn and develop, based on the contributions of the giver. Teachers, by the nature of the profession, reach out beyond themselves to their students, colleagues, and schools in general, recognizing the needs of others and accommodating those, in addition to their own. The assumption of the study, that candidates enter the PDS program at the second level of the hierarchy, wanting to belong to the group of candidates with whom they learn about teaching and learning. The goal of the PDS program, to develop candidates from the belonging to self-actualization and possibly transcendent level, when measured, finds basis in documents that require reflection, self-examination, and critique by candidates.

Results of the analysis suggested trends in development from belonging toward self-actualization. Email conversations in the first part of the year clearly supported the supposition that candidates needed to belong to the group. Candidates mentioned on numerous occasions the importance of having a candidate support system that "helped them through" their internship. The importance of friends dominated the exchanges of self-reflection and positioning into the role of teacher, suggesting that their identity aligns with Maslow's second level of need. As assignments of lesson planning, observation analysis, tutoring projects, and portfolios came due, the language turned to a higher level of esteem, whereby the candidates projected a sense of dependence on university instructors and supervisors to determine their identity. Candidates acquiesced responsibility for their formation, entrusting it instead to outside influences, instructors and supervisors.

A shift in identify formation occurred during the exit interview that centered on the final portfolio. This document, developed by candidates for the purpose of reflecting on their development toward becoming a teacher, uses the INTASC Standards as the basis for comparing artifact collections and justification. At the exit level, the portfolio includes a four-component collection of: plans, implementation of plans, documentation of response, and reflection on the process. Candidates, when probed about the relationship of the portfolio development process and their perception of themselves as teachers, overwhelmingly confirmed that they saw themselves as teachers when they used the portfolio as a lens to make that determination. Qualitative analysis of the data revealed a group of candidates who saw themselves as teachers, albeit not completely clear as to what that meant in operational terms. The candidates overwhelmingly agreed that the assignment to develop a portfolio at the exit point seemed redundant and tedious, following fourteen weeks of student teaching, but recognized the importance of stopping to reflect, self-critique, and examine their identity as a teacher from the perspective of their work in the portfolio.

The results of this study led to decisions regarding the preparation of mentor teachers as supporters of the portfolio process. Conversations with candidates suggested that mentor teachers influence their continued commitment to teaching as a profession. The modeling, support, and acceptance by mentor teachers encourages candidates to persevere in spite of the difficulties to form their own identities as teachers. However, often mentor teachers disparage the portfolio as useless, since many claim that no one will look at them during job interviews. To encourage support for the process, mentor teachers reviewed data generated from this study and worked toward changing practice of discouragement to encouragement of the reflective, self-critique, and examination inherent in the portfolio process. The potential for mentor teacher self-reflective practices as a component of the PDS seemed more likely than prior to this study.

Arts-Based

In the fifth year of the program, the team of instructors of the PDS methods courses developed a unit of study on the Mayan culture, as a United Nations recognized indigenous group. The instructor group created a teacher resource package of information about the Mayan culture in the form of: artifacts representing the geography of the area, art and architecture related to the Mayan culture's perspective of geometry, a photograph journal of geological formations in Mayan areas, and a multi-genre writing project about the Mayan culture and the lives of Mayan people. For four weeks during the semester, the mathematics, science, social studies, and language arts courses guided candidates through the study of geometry, geography, geology, and multi-genre writing, demonstrating the instructional use of the materials in the instructor-developed teacher resource package. Throughout the presentations, candidates began the process of exploring their own U.N. topic from which to draw and develop a teacher resource packet, inclusive of artifacts of geographical reference, art and architectural pieces with geometric understanding embedded, photographs of geological information relevant to the topic, and multigenre written pieces, explaining the topic.

Data collected included multiple forms of electronic and personal, verbal communication. Email communication between instructors and candidates on the development of the topic provided information on the process candidates used to think through their choices. These communications led candidates to understand the depth, the value for future teaching, and the use of the project as an exercise in developing integrated packets of information. Other electronic information included the finished candidate-developed teacher research packet, which included art pieces for each of the four areas of study. Personal, verbal communication consisted of conversations between instructors and candidates, before, during, or after classes.

Data review employed the constructs of artful teaching. Artful teaching principles designate that teachers apply techniques used by artists in their teaching practice. Artists develop their art through a process of: (1) a desire to create, (2) inspiration, (3) technique development, (4) self-criticism and doubt, and (5) rigorous refining until the product emerges as art. Artists use art to portray the human condition. Likewise, art reflects the human condition as beautiful, macabre, intriguing, and/or thought provoking. Art developed employing the five processes, engages the viewer, reader, listener of the art. Artful teachers use the processes employed by artists when developing integrated information, designing instruction, and/or implementing plans.

The data collected were analyzed through the five processes of art development to determine the level of artful creation of the projects. A direct relationship developed between language in electronic and verbal communications and artful practices and products. In essence, candidates whose language exhibited the five components of the artful process, including self-criticism and rigorous refining, produced artful resource packages. In contrast, candidates whose language exhibited concern for external controls, such as grades, and pressure to produce something for which they saw no value to them directly, exhibiting little or no artful processing, netted less than artful products. Findings served as guideposts for instructors to reconvene and reconsider the instructional approach in courses, so that candidates not only experienced the art, but understood artful practices in developing packages for later planning and learning.

Ethnographic

A doctoral student serving as co-coordinator for the PDS cadre, within the context of the doctoral dissertation, sought to determine the influence of school ecology (physical surroundings, formal policies and rules, resources) and culture (attitudes, cultural norms, and relationships), on the management of stress by first year teachers. Participants in the study included twelve first-year teachers, former PDS candidates, working in the PDS setting as first year teachers, and twenty randomly selected first year teachers hired into the same district whose teacher preparation varied. The two years spanned the year of PDS and the first year of teaching. During the first year, interviews, email communications, and portfolio entries provided data. During the second year, interviews, email communications, observations at first year teacher staff development, observations of teaching, and general conversations served as data sources.

In ethnographic work, the researcher goes through phases of entry into the culture of the group under study. In this study, the researcher taught the twelve PDS candidates during the instructional phase of the program, met weekly in seminars during the second half, and attended the first year teacher staff development meetings as an observer. During the second year, the researcher observed, conversed, interviewed, and spent considerable time in the classrooms of the twelve teachers. In addition, in the second year, the researcher changed roles from observer to participant-observer. In this capacity, the researcher conducted focus group interviews among the non-PDS graduate first year teachers regarding the stressors of first year teaching within the context of ecology and culture of their schools. Also, in the new capacity, the researcher observed and participated in the PDS graduates' classrooms.

The results of the study suggested that an understanding of ecology and culture affected first year teachers' management of stress. PDS candidates employed in schools of their PDS internship, showed higher competence levels in the management of stress. Their understanding of the ecology and culture of the schools, enhanced by their prior involvement in the school, lessened their need to manage stress. However, PDS candidates who accepted jobs in schools outside the PDS cadre, showed lower levels of stress management capability. In spite of these lowered levels, PDS graduates, as first year teachers, showed overall higher levels of stress management capability than first year teachers who underwent other forms of teacher preparation. PDS candidates, employed in unfamiliar schools, knew the culture and ecology of the district, which aided in their somewhat reduced stress management capacity. Analysis revealed that PDS candidates, accustomed to flexible schedules and experiences as team members in the PDS, adjusted more readily to the demands of learning a foreign ecological and cultural setting. In contrast, first year teachers prepared otherwise, expressed limited understanding of the ecology and culture, and exhibited high levels of stress in their new, unfamiliar setting.

The trend in hiring graduates of the PDS program by the district has steadily moved upward from eight percent, in the first year, to twenty-five percent in the fourth year. The value of having an assemblage of so many graduates in one district, the expertise they lend from having lived the experience and the willingness to share their experiences with incoming candidates, supports the program. The caution lies in the willingness to show flexibility, should the program adjust and change. The value in having so many graduates in the district that served as their preparation ground, the understanding of the culture and ecology of the district, reduces the stress related to first year teacher induction, thereby ostensibly increasing the probability of retention. This trend signaled caution to the first year teacher staff development program, which had to rethink its design to accommodate teacher inductees who knew and embraced the district. The stressors moved from the first year teacher to the first year teacher staff development programs, requiring change and adjustment. This study began anew and is under way.

SUMMARY OF THE RELATIONSHIP BETWEEN RESEARCH AND THE STANDARD

The developing stage of the NCATE PDS Standards shows trends in two areas: shared responsibility and research-based decision-making. The seven studies outlined in this chapter demonstrate these principles. The studies show how multiple members of the team contributed to research in and of the program. The studies also demonstrate how the research findings contributed to changes in the program and further research. The essence of the developing stage embodied in these studies, serve as examples of research at this level of development. An in depth account of how each study addresses the expectation of this level of the standard follows.

In the quasi-experimental study, the decision to begin the research initiated from a need identified by school personnel. The bonds of trust, established after three years of team-based program development between university and school leadership, provided the basis for pursuing the project. The results of the first year's study provided the impetus to continue research on the effect of tutoring on student achievement. The cycle of renewing research, based on findings, suggests that this PDS uses research-based decision making to continually improve both student and candidate performance. Shared responsibility, apparent in the movement of idea from the principals to the methods class to the tutoring clusters, suggests a team approach to the problem of student needs in mathematics achievement.

The case study, an assigned project for completion of the masters' program, thrust the mentor teacher into a position of engaging multiple members of the PDS program in the process of conducting the action research/case study. The shared responsibility of many groups in the constituency provided the data needed to document the use of interpersonal intelligence during reading and writing time. By sharing the data collection among several others, the teacher acquired a much broader perspective of the situation in her classroom. The support and guidance of the university coordinator, not the teacher of record for the project, provided the expertise the mentor teacher needed to develop and complete the project. The success of the case study occurred as a result of shared responsibility. Based on the findings, the teacher elected to change her practice, supporting the principle of research-based decision making.

The survey research study, initiated by the site coordinator, provided on-going documentation of the progress of the PDS program toward a high performing team. The contributions of all constituents to the data pool increased the credence of the findings, which over time suggested that the program progressed toward a high performing team. The data in early years suggested the need for adjustments in programming, when implementation increased the level of perception by constituents that the program performed at a very high level because the constituents understood the purpose, felt empowered, held good relationships, sensed flexibility, worked at the optimal level, felt recognized, and maintained a high morale. In essence, the results spurred the group to higher levels of team performance, toward a transformational level.

Due to the trends in colleges of education toward the use of portfolio to demonstrate program excellence, a rich, vast collection of data avails itself to PDS researchers. The philosophical study conducted in the PDS program tied field experiences to university coursework through the portfolio, but more significantly, to the deeper investigation of the students' perceptions of themselves as developing teachers. The shared responsibility of the portfolio development, reflection, and subsequent philosophic discussion, fell to the university personnel and candidate. The research findings, however, indicated a need to extend the shared responsibility to mentor teachers, who influence candidates, due to the common experience of teaching the same children during the field experience.

Arts based research, an untapped method in PDS research, invokes a need for an understanding of the principles associated with arts based thinking and learning. The study described in the chapter refers to a shared project among university instructors. The shared responsibility of developing the component parts of the package relates to the expectations of the standard. Likewise, the findings suggest that the data led instructors to re-examine their practice to engage more students on a higher level of artistic thought. Collaboration among instructors who share mutual groups of students, infrequent in many university settings, supported the principle of shared responsibility.

The ethnographic study included in the collection aligns with the conventions of ethnographic methods: extensive time in the field and increased access to the culture under study from observer to participant. This study aligned with the expectations of the standard on both counts. The district first year teacher staff development program personnel permitted the university researcher, a doctoral student affiliated with the program, to enter the program as an observer, and over time, embraced a more active role as participant-observer. The first year teachers and their school administrators joined in the process of studying the management of stress by first year graduates of the PDS program. The findings from the study led to decision-making by the first year teacher staff development team, since graduates of the PDS program sponsored by the district represented one quarter of the training population in the second year of the study.

In all of the hypothetical studies, the essence of the standard maintained and guided the PDS program's research agenda. Potentially, the PDS program changes and continues to develop toward an at standard stage when using research-based decisions. However, essential to progression to the next level, are shared responsibility of all constituents to conduct research and use the findings for decisions. Although university personnel traditionally initiate and conduct research on behalf of the PDS program, functioning at this level and progression to the next requires a shift in paradigm toward inclusion of all constituents in the research process. This suggests a team development approach to the management of the PDS program.

REFERENCES

Blanchard, K., P. Zigarmi, and D Zigarmi. *Leadership and the One Minute Manager-Increasing Effectiveness through Situational Leadership*. New York William Morrow and Company, 1985.

Gardner, Howard. *Frames of Mind: The Theory of Multiple Intelligences*. New York: Basic Books, 1983.

Chapter Eight

PDS Research at the At Standard Stage

An at standard PDS program, one that has arrived at a high level of perform-ance, embodies principles of unparalleled shared teaming. In this mode of op-eration, based on the language of the standard's description, constituents share leadership on each others' boards, form groups of decision makers from all constituent groups, and make agreements that all partners engender PDS as essential to their planning and operation. This progressed stage of devel-opment requires extensive levels of trust and shared understanding that em-body boundary spanning for everyone. When a PDS program reaches the at standard developmental stage, the term "our" PDS program becomes opera-tive for all constituents at the university, school, district, community, and par-ent levels. This strongly cultivated, committed group stands poised to account to its public entities for its effect on learning across for P-12, candidates, teachers, and the professoriate.

According to the NCATE PDS Standards, at standard PDS programs be-come responsible and accountable to public entities that include: parents, uni-versities, schools, districts, state and federal agencies. Parents, concerned that their children receive the best education, require assurances that external in-terventions, such as PDS, benefit rather than detract from their children's ed-ucation. Universities and colleges of education, under continuous scrutiny by state and federal agencies, require guarantees that teacher preparation pro-grams, with the intensity and commitment of PDS, produce teacher candi-dates of a higher caliber than those generated from other preparation pro-grams. Schools and school districts under continuous pressure and scrutiny to produce high levels of performance by children need warranties of some sort that the programs they have put in place will sustain, in spite of the additional commitment to PDS. The at standard PDS, because of its tightly woven mutual bond, can provide the impetus needed to pose research questions and provide answers to these in a systematic, reasonable way that establishes understanding and continued trust.

Specifically, the standards state that at standard PDS programs do the following regarding inquiry and the use of the results of inquiry to inform, improve, and change, to the betterment of all learners:

- Practice in the PDS and partnering university is inquiry-based and an inquiry orientation weaves together learning, accountability, and faculty development.
- Inquiry is used routinely at an individual classroom, departmental, and school-wide level (at school and university) to inform decisions about which approaches to teaching and learning work best.
- Inquiry-based practice sits at the intersection of professional education reform and school improvement. Because the professional preparation program and the school both view the PDS partnership as integral to their individual purposes, the PDS partnership leverages significant change.
- Through the process of asking and answering questions, partners examine whether and how much the PDS partnership increases learning for all. A continuous process of assessment and evaluation based on local, state, and national standards is integrated into the PDS partnership, resulting in continual refinement of practices and increased professionalism.

These expectations indicate a PDS program that performs for the benefit of all involved. The at standard PDS constituents understand that through questioning and studying the operation of the program, all members improve and develop on a higher level. Through systematic approaches to inquiry (research), learning is more clearly understood. In addition, change, based on inquiry, leads decisions for all constituent groups.

Research-driven decision making, resulting from inquiry-based approaches to PDS operations, according to the at standard level of the standards, then leads to changes in policies. According to the language of the standards:

- By integrating their expertise and knowledge of practice, PDS partners develop new approaches for examining and improving the practices of individuals and the policies of both institutions.
- Changes in policy and practice contemplated by PDS partner institutions are routinely filtered through the lens of the PDS partnership.
- They use their analyses to make constructive changes at the individual, institutional, and partnership levels.

Finally, with changes in place and policies adjusted to accommodate all constituent groups, the at standard PDS program reports to its public entities:

- PDS partners provide the public with evidence about what faculty, candidates, and P-12 students know and are able to do, and the values and commitments toward which PDS partners and candidates are disposed.
- PDS partners develop the capacity to take knowledge-based action by regularly collecting information about the ways in which individuals' practices and institutional policies affect the achievement of P-12 students.
- As PDS partners systematically examine results related to how well, how much and which P-12 students, candidates, faculty, and other professionals are learning, they begin a process of continuous assessment, reflection, and action that results in continuous improvement of learning for all PDS participants.
- PDS partners use their shared work to improve outcomes for P-12 students, candidates, faculty, and other professionals.
- PDS partners and candidates systematically analyze data to address the gaps in achievement among racial groups.

The language of the standard at this level suggests a strong commitment to maintain an open, transparent approach to maintaining the PDS program. The maintenance, supported through inquiry and research, data collection, analysis, and dissemination suggests a high performing team.

TEAM DEVELOPMENT—PERFORMING

The at standard PDS, a fully functional program, with high levels of trust, embodies the performing level of the team development model. At this level, team members function at a very high level, working together, trusting at a very high level, accomplishing intended goals, and measuring these through inquiry and continuous examination. Research in a performing atmosphere requires a supportive leadership style to guide the team through processes and procedures for completing research initiatives. As teachers, candidates, professors, district personnel, and others work toward understanding the PDS program through research, those with research expertise, support the effort with research expertise, data processing, and venues for presenting findings from studies. A transformative style of leadership carries the at standard group through the situational moments of keeping the group together as the group changes, reports, and develops.

DIMENSIONS OF RESEARCH

Research dimensions at this stage embody the highest levels of design considerations and are achievable, due to the high levels of involvement of constituents in each others' educational settings. *Research problems* reflect concerns about achievement for all, including students, candidates, teachers, professors, schools, districts, etc. The at standard *setting*, poised to study and produce plans that encourage development and growth, provides an environment organized and ready for experimental research designs. *Settings* at this stage include the inside of classrooms, both in the school and the university, comparisons of PDS programs to others, etc. *Research investigators*, in a well developed collaborative include mentor teachers, possibly as MAT or M.Ed. students at the university, university personnel, doctoral students serving as PDS coordinators or mentor teachers, doctoral students interested in PDS, and teacher candidates participating in all manner of research, including experimental research. *Research methods* possibilities encompass all designs, due to the high levels of trust and recognition of members' contributions to the process. At this level experimental research seems the most poignant, due to the comparative nature of experimental designs, the trust levels that allow randomization, and the knowledge that findings garnered from the research serve to benefit and move educational achievement to a higher level. To achieve an experimental study, random groups, tested in blind studies, require the high level of trust and group functioning that occurs at this stage of development. At the initiation of the No Child Left Behind legislation, federal funding for research encouraged, at times insisted, that educational research employ experimental designs. However, following an examination of PDS levels of development, it becomes apparent, that until a level of trust emerges, resulting from shared leadership, the potential for experimental work remains theoretical and elusive. The *purpose of research* at this level, to ascertain the effect of PDS on achievement, eventually leads to reports that support policy changes, which then support further research and continued development.

MATCHED METHODS OF AERA RESEARCH AND NCATE AT STANDARD STAGE

The seven methods of research discussed and represented in Chapter Seven also apply to the at standard level of PDS development. The hypothetical studies noted in Chapter Seven do not differ from the approach taken at this level, and therefore will not be reconstructed in this chapter. The emphasis in this chapter, the experimental design focuses control over all factors that may affect the result of an experiment. In doing this, the researcher attempts to determine or predict what may occur. Experimental design, a blueprint of the procedure that enables the researcher to test his hypothesis by reaching valid conclusions about relationships between independent and dependent variables. It refers to the conceptual framework within which the experiment is conducted (p. 1).

Critical to the success of experimental research, randomization, requires that researchers select or assign participants to experimental and control groups. Participants in experimental studies, randomly selected or randomly assigned to experimental and control groups, represent samples from a population. Certain assumptions placed on sampled groups presume that samples represent the population and that each participant had an equal opportunity to participate in either experimental or control groups. Experimental control attempts to predict events that will occur in the experimental setting by neutralizing the effects of other factors (p. 2)

In addition to considerations for randomization and control for manipulation of the independent variable, threats to internal and external validity bear consideration. Internal validity asks, did the experimental treatment make the difference in this specific instance rather than other extraneous variables? External validity asks, to what populations, settings, treatment variables, and measurement variables can this observed effect be generalized? Factors threatening internal validity include: history, maturation, pre-testing, measuring instruments, regression, statistical regression, differential selection, experimental mortality, or a combination of several factors. Factors threatening external validity/generalization include: pre-testing, differential selection, experimental procedures, and multiple-treatment interference. These factors, controlled by randomization, pre-testing, control groups, and additional groups, raise the level of generalizability due to the multiple controls placed on the factors influencing validity.

True experimental designs, three in total, range in effectiveness to control for internal and external validity concerns. The Pretest Posttest Control Group design includes the following blueprint: random selection/assignment of participants to experimental or control groups, pretest, treatment or intervention for the experimental group, and a posttest for each group. This design controls for most factors of internal and external validity, with the exception of pre-testing and multiple treatment. The Solomon four-group design begins with the components of the pretest posttest control group design, but adds two other levels that include: (1) treatment and posttest, (2) posttest only. These additional groups control for the effect of pre-testing, making this design the most powerful of the three, since all factors, other than multiple treatment are controlled for in this design. Finally, the Posttest Only control group design, used when a situation cannot be pre-tested, but grouping by randomization remains an option, controls for several factors of internal and external validity, exclusive of pre-testing, multiple treatments, differential selection, experimental mortality, and procedures.

These three designs, though elegant and answer the question of causation due to the controls placed on variability, challenge educational researchers due to the random selection/assignment required. Most schools, under pressure to produce like test scores for all populations, find experimental work daunting. However, the at standard PDS program, as described by the NCATE PDS Standards, maintains a high level of trust that allows randomization to occur more readily. The three scenarios described below represent examples of hypothetical studies in PDS settings that represent the three true experimental designs.

Pretest Posttest Design Sample

Teachers in the PDS program worked with university personnel for years to encourage candidates to conduct action research. Many of the candidates (interns) did not see the value in conducting action research, thereby lowering the quality of the projects proposed and action research conducted. Most of the mentor teachers did not know what constituted action research, nor how it informed instructional practice and improvement. Consequently, candidate action research projects met with limited support, at times scorn, eventually deteriorating to assignment completion, rather than a project that inspires and encourages the practice of continuous inquiry. In spite of this, the university continued to assign action research as a required project for PDS candidates.

At an annual planning meeting, the mentor teacher leadership team began to inquire as to why the action research project was required and what could the university replace the project with to provide the candidates with a "real world" experience. After some discussion, university personnel explained that the purpose of the project, to encourage candidates to use careful inquiry and reflective practice, both as candidates, but eventually as teachers, leads to stronger teaching. A deeper discussion following the administration of the Intern Support Inventory (ISI), revealed that most mentor teachers did not understand the process or benefits of action research, nor how to support candidates' use of action research. To heighten both awareness and garner support for candidates' action research projects, an experimental study of the use of action research by teachers and their level of support for candidates ensued.

The purpose of the study was to enhance support for candidates' action research projects. The research question was posed: How does the use of action research by teachers, to change instructional practice, affect teacher support of interns' action research projects? It was hypothesized that mentor teachers who used action research in their classrooms would differ significantly at the .05 level, on ISI, from teachers who did not use action research. The level of use of action research by teachers served as the independent variable. The level of support observed on the ISI served as the dependent variable.

The method of inquiry required multiple steps. Annually, all mentor teachers attended mentor teacher preparation meetings. The meetings, conducted by the teacher leadership team, provided information about the instructional expectations and field experiences for candidates. In addition, the meeting provided mentor teachers with guidance and methods for supporting candidates in both the observation and practical parts of the candidates' preparation in their classrooms. At the meetings, all teachers were trained in the use of action research. The training included tools for developing, conducting, and analyzing data from action research projects, with the intent of changing practice. Teachers were informed that they were expected to conduct their action research projects when they returned to their campuses.

Hall and Hord, in *Implementing Change: Patterns, Principles, and Potholes,* note that the likelihood of implementation of new practices presented in staff development, less than 3% with only expectations for implementations, but increases to 97% when continued support ensues. From among the 100 teachers involved in the PDS, fifty teachers were randomly selected to participate in a study of the use of action research. All teachers were administered the ISI as a pretest to determine the level of support for action research. Twenty-five teachers were randomly assigned to an experimental group and twenty-five to a control group. The experimental group met with university personnel and a team of doctoral student assistants on a monthly basis to further develop, discuss, encourage, and follow the use of the teacher-designed action research project. University personnel assisted teachers in the experimental group with data collection, data analysis, and development of action plans for instructional change. The control group met occasionally to inform the team of its progress on completing its action research. These ad hoc information meetings, held at the behest of the control group teachers during their planning times, after school, or other teacher convenient times, consisted primarily of teachers in the control group informing university personnel of their progress. Throughout the semester long project, candidates continued to complete university requirements to conduct action research.

At the conclusion of fifteen weeks, all fifty teachers completed the ISI as a posttest. Data from the pre and posttests were analyzed using an ANCOVA. The pretest served as a covariate to determine whether the control and experimental groups differed significantly. The data revealed no significant differences, at the .05 level, between the groups at the pretest level, indicating that randomization created like groups. However, the analysis of variance of the posttests revealed significant differences at the .05 level, implying that the experimental group more strongly supported the use of action research in the classroom. It was concluded that the intervention of strong, continuous support for teacher-developed action research projects enhances teacher support for action research conducted by candidates.

This study supported the theory that doing leads to learning. Because the teachers conducted their own action research projects, albeit supported by university personnel, their understanding and recognition of the value of action research transformed to higher levels of support of candidates' action research projects. The results of the study imply that university personnel, eager to create excellent teachers through action research inquiry methods, increase the potential of the effect of action research projects by supporting teachers' action research projects.

Solomon Four-Group Design Sample

The district that collaborated with the university to form the PDS program changed in demographics over a period of ten years, to include 40 percent increase in children living in poverty. In addition, state mandates for success on high stakes writing exams for all subpopulations, yielded a 30 percent decreased passing rate, particularly among children on free and reduced meals. This phenomenon led to a deeper examination of the failure rate as related to current instructional practices. The district school improvement planning team, consisting of teachers, district administrative personnel, and university PDS coordinators, met to discuss collaborative means to approach the dilemma. The resulting plan included an experimental study of support for instructional practices.

The purpose of the study was to increase writing scores of fourth and seventh grade students as measured by state mandated tests. The research question was posed: What is the effect of tutoring by PDS candidates on fourth and seventh grade writing scores? It was hypothesized that students receiving tutoring in writing by PDS candidates would differ significantly, at the .05 level, from students who did not receive tutoring from a PDS candidate. Tutoring served as the independent variable. Scores on state mandated tests served as the dependent variable.

During the annual PDS team meeting, district personnel, including district leadership, building administrators, and teachers expressed concern that many students' writing scores on the state mandated exams fell below state and national expectations, thereby lowering the state ranking of the district. In spite of the overall district general lack of success, one school in the district garnered 100 percent passage on the writing test for two consecutive years. A team of teachers, from the successful school, worked in concert to develop writing skills at the grade level tested, using writing theories that suggest discourse among writers leads to excellence in writing. Following several years of theory testing, all students consistently excelled in writing. The program grew from the upper grades to the lower, until the entire school engaged in the discourse-based writing program. When asked if this program could transfer to other campuses, the lead teacher in the project, a doctoral student at the university, agreed to use this opportunity to develop her dissertation into an experimental study of the program in other settings to determine the transferability of the program.

The doctoral student, in partnership with her advisor, a PDS coordinator, solicited the assistance of university personnel connected to the PDS program. The design of the study included the use of PDS candidates as observers of the discourse-writing project. The candidates' role, to chronicle the delivery of the program, provided curricular-fidelity data, general discourse among students, and teacher discourse with the students, to the researcher. As part of the collaboration, the language arts instructor agreed to: work with the teachers who had developed the writing program, adjust university instruction to prepare candidates as observers of discourse in a writing class, the underpinnings of the discourse-writing theory, and monitor candidates' record keeping as they observed teachers' practice of the method. The rhetoric instructors from the university college of arts and science agreed to: work with the school district to learn the state and local scoring rubric systems, serve as evaluators of the students' writing at pretest and posttest points, and assist candidates in evaluating writing. Due to the high level of trust in the at standard PDS, a research protocol developed to study the effectiveness of the writing program on student achievement in writing, led to an experimental research design.

The PDS school with the greatest need for intervention, as measured by consistent failures in writing for four consecutive years, was selected for implementation of the program. Students in the school attended all classes in block groups. Following several years of failure in writing, the school created a separate block of time specifically for writing. Four teachers taught the writing sections, which at the time of the study's initiation, followed no systematic approach to writing instruction and netted equal failure rates from all four teachers. To date, no systematic study of the four instructional settings revealed cause for failure. Since the teachers all maintained highly qualified teacher status, due to completion of degrees in education and state certification testing, teaching was dismissed as the greatest indicator of failure. The school determined that the methods employed could be greater influence, so were willing to engage in experimentation to test this assumption.

The school agreed to study the cause and effect of the discourse-writing project on student writing achievement. The only proviso, that all children receive the benefit of the program, prompted some negotiating. To accommodate the concern for equity and ethics, the doctoral student agreed to present the program to the other 60 students during a second 12-week session in the spring. For the purpose of this study, the four teachers were randomly assigned to instruct one of four groups, and 120 students were randomly assigned, with thirty to each group, to serve as subjects in one of the four groups. The two teachers randomly assigned to employ the discourse-writing method (Groups 1 and 2), met with the doctoral student during the summer to develop their skills in using the discourse-writing method. The other two teachers met with the doctoral student to describe their methods of teaching writing. The doctoral student listened and encouraged the teachers to continue with their practices.

The Solomon four-group design was used to study the effect of the use of the discourse-writing approach on student achievement in writing. The Solomon four-group design creates two groups that receive treatment and two that do not. A diagram of the design is shown in table 8.1.

Group 1 students were administered the state writing prompt as a pretest, received instruction from their teacher using the discourse-writing method (supported by the doctoral student), and were administered the identical posttest following twelve weeks of intervention. Group 2 students received instruction from a second teacher who used the discourse-writing method for twelve weeks (supported by the doctoral student), then completed the state writing prompt. Group 3 students responded to the state writing prompt, attended writing class, then completed the posttest. Group 4 students attended writing class taught by a teacher who chose the approach to writing instruction, and responded to the state writing prompt at the end of the 12-week program. The pretests of Groups 1 and 3 were scored by the arts and science faculty, applying the state rubric for scoring writing.

During the implementation of the 12-week study, candidates used a Discourse Analysis Checklist to record the discourse of the children during all four writing sessions. The checklist consisted of discourse behaviors common to the discourse-writing method. Discourse between students, be-

Table 8.1.   A Solomon Four-Group Design

Group 1	R	X	O	X
Group 2	R		O	X
Group 3	R	X		X
Group 4	R			X

tween students and the teachers, and discourse with themselves as they wrote, were observed and noted by candidates. Candidates submitted weekly reports to the language arts instructor, indicating their observations of the discourse. The language arts instructor guided the candidates to careful observation and chronicling. Each candidate rotated through all four classes, three times, across the twelve weeks. At the end of the observation period, the candidates prepared a report of the observations across the four instructional settings that described their perceptions of writing skill development of the children while comparing the four settings. Throughout the process, the candidates remained uninformed about which instructional setting used the discourse-writing methods and which did not.

At the end of the twelve weeks, all data were collected and analyzed. At this point, all 120 students were administered the state released writing test. The arts and science faculty scored the exams and worked with the candidates to understand the scoring system and their reasoning for assigning the scores. The doctoral student worked with the language arts instructor to analyze the trends observed from the Discourse Analysis Checklist data for the purposes of determining at what level of fidelity the teachers assigned to the experimental groups taught the discourse-writing method. At the end of the study, all four teachers were surveyed regarding their perceptions of the students' writing ability and predictions for success on the state mandated writing exam.

Posttest data were analyzed using an ANOVA to determine differences across groups. Analysis revealed there were significant differences at the .05 level. A post-hoc Tukey test for variability was conducted to determine where differences occurred and revealed that the two experimental groups scored significantly higher than students in the control groups. The within group differences were not significant, suggesting that the groups were homogenous and implying that the randomization created like groups, thus further supporting the findings.

The checklist data revealed interesting trends across the four classes. The data were analyzed using an ANOVA to determine differences in the levels of discourse in the four classes. Significant differences, at the .05 level, were noted across the groups. A Tukey post-hoc analysis revealed that the experimental groups had significantly higher scores than the two control groups. The two experimental groups, supported by the doctoral student throughout the twelve weeks, showed significantly higher levels of discourse, at the .05 level, among students, with teachers, and with themselves. The Group 3 control group had slightly higher levels of discourse than Group 4 control group, but still significantly lower than the experimental groups. It was assumed that the pretest influenced the Group 3 teacher to experiment with instruction, based on the fact that these students were seemingly under study due to the pre-testing.

Data from the survey were analyzed using an ANOVA to determine differences in teachers' perceptions of future student success on writing measures. There were no significant differences observed among the four teachers. It was noted that all four teachers thought their students would succeed on the state mandated test and their methods were sound enough to foster that success. The finding suggests that teachers' perceptions of their teaching excellence were high. Several implications for change in instructional practice emerged.

This study demonstrated the effectiveness of the discourse-writing method and its transferability to additional settings. However, the method best transferred with considerable guidance from the experimental researcher. Therefore, the influence of the experimenter should be considered as an influence on the cause of the effect. Further research on the effectiveness of the method would require less intervention by the researcher on the implementation of the treatment. However, at this level of experimentation and PDS program, coupled with the fears associated with failures in writing due to threats of the removal of funds, support for the use of a new method seemed logical. The next step in studying the method would be to train the teachers in the method, then trust that teacher preparation would sustain change and support differences in learning.

Posttest Only Design Sample

Due to the cost of PDS programs to universities and the low instructor to student ratio, the university that sponsored the PDS and standard certification/placement pre-service program, began to examine the cost-effectiveness of the PDS. The at standard PDS program under scrutiny found itself under pressure to demonstrate that PDS effectively serves learning at the P-12 level while retaining teachers with positive attitudes toward teaching. The coordinator of the PDS program, a tenure-track assistant professor, proposed a longitudinal study that compared the PDS program to the standard certification/placement pre-service program offered by the college of education. The purpose of the study, to examine three aspects of program success: (1) teacher retention, (2) student academic achievement, and (3) attitude toward teaching, led to an experimental study that compared the three outcomes between two groups of candidates with differing teacher preparation methods. The research question: Do PDS and standard student teacher placement programs differ significantly, at the .05 level, on three indicators, retention, achievement, and attitude? It was hypothesized that the groups would differ significantly and that the PDS program would be higher in all three categories.

No pretest measures retention, academic success of students, and attitude toward teaching; therefore, a posttest only control group experimental design supported the research. Candidates entered the teacher preparation program in the college of education, unaware of the differences between standard student teaching placement and PDS programs. Each program produced approximately fifty prepared teachers annually. Of the one hundred candidates who entered the program, fifty were randomly assigned to study in the standard certification/placement pre-service program and fifty were randomly assigned to participate in the PDS program.

The two programs differed on several points. Candidates in the standard certification/placement pre-service program completed a degree in a field of study, generally in the college of arts and science. In the last two years of their degree program, candidates entered a teacher preparation program. In that program, candidates studied child development, perspectives of education, methods of instruction, and classroom management, coupled with 60 hours of observations in the field. In the last semester of the senior year, the candidates were placed in the field to student teach for a semester with teachers in the field who may or may not have known they were expected to supervise a student teacher. A supervisor from the university met with the candidates for one hour before placement. At the end of twelve weeks the candidates graduated and sought teaching jobs.

In contrast, the candidates assigned to the PDS program entered the program as a cohort. These students had completed their arts and science requirements, completing a degree in a field of study. They entered the PDS program in their last two years. Every semester for these two years they spent time in the field, comparing theory to practice between their courses of child development, perspectives of education, methods of instruction, and classroom management. The university and school personnel worked collaboratively to create a community that embraced the candidates as both learners and contributors to the process of teacher preparation. In the last two semesters, the field experience increased to the point where the candidates completely took over teaching in a classroom where brokered agreements between candidates, mentor teachers, and supervisors provided the candidates with the support needed to transition from university instruction to teaching. The candidates met weekly for seminars which they designed and presented to each other, and at their behest, involved mentor teachers, building administrators, district, and university personnel. After twelve weeks the candidates graduated and sought teaching jobs.

Before graduation, all 90 candidates who completed the program reported to the researcher their job placements and signed a waiver that allowed the researcher to track their retention, state mandated student achievement on standardized measures, and attitude toward teaching for five years. At this time, the researcher obtained permission, from the four districts employing the candidates to track the 80 candidates who accepted teaching positions, on the three variables of retention, academic success, and attitude toward teaching. Forty-five candidates from the PDS program entered the field, whereas thirty-five from the standard program entered at the same time. For five years the researcher tracked the retention of the candidates as teachers by perusing the district employee website as well as continuous communication with candidates/teachers. The four districts annually provided aggregate achievement scores in mathematics and reading for each teacher employed from the university program. Finally, all candidate/teachers completed attitude scales on a secure, anonymous program that required a password, known only to the respondent but served as the tracking device for completed surveys. The instrument allowed the researcher to know who had and had not completed the annual survey but did not disclose which respondent completed which survey. The data were treated according to the type: retention, nominal; achievement, interval; and survey, interval. The number of candidate/teachers in the field teaching across the five years constituted retention data and were analyzed using an F-test. The F-test yields a one-tailed probability that the variances in the PDS and standard program are not significantly different. The analysis of the data across five years for the two groups revealed a significant difference at the .05 level.

Student achievement data for mathematics and reading, presented in aggregate form, yielded different findings. Of the eighty original candidates/ teachers in the pool, twenty taught in grade levels that did not require mandated state testing in mathematics and reading. Of the twenty, twelve graduated from the PDS program and eight from the standard program. Consequently, test data from thirty-three PDS candidate/teachers and twenty-seven standard candidate/teachers were analyzed. The data were reported in percentage of students passing the test in both mathematics and reading across the remaining sixty candidates/teachers. The data were analyzed using an ANOVA. The analysis resulted in no significant differences between groups in either instructional area. However, a more careful examination of the data revealed mean passing rates of 80 percent and 85 percent of students from the standard and PDS candidate/teacher cohorts, respectively. Although no significant differences were observed, the high level of passing rates suggests that teacher preparation had no significant effect on student achievement in mathematics and reading.

Surveys from candidate teachers, completed annually, provided interval data, and when analyzed using a factor analysis, revealed trends in candidates/

teachers' attitudes toward teaching. Among teachers trained in the standard program, results indicated a growing negative attitude toward teaching with over 70 percent of the variance accounted for in three variables: job dissatisfaction, peer workload sharing, and communication with administrators. Among teachers trained in the PDS program, over 80 percent of the variance related to job satisfaction, concern for student success, and new knowledge and skill acquisition that would lead to improved teaching. The factor loading of the two groups demonstrates a significant difference in attitude toward teaching between the two groups.

This longitudinal study provided the university and school system with important data for making decisions regarding teacher preparation and the investment of both university and school system involved in the shared process. Two of the three data sets analyzed suggest that teacher retention and attitude toward teaching are more clearly apparent among candidates/teachers prepared under the PDS program. The lack of differences in test scores suggests that placement in programs has little, if any effect of program placement on student achievement in mathematics and reading. Since passing rates for both groups of teacher preparation candidates/teachers were very high, it seems logical that the PDS program appears preferable due to the high retention rate and positive attitudes toward teaching.

SUMMARY OF THE RELATIONSHIP BETWEEN RESEARCH AND THE STANDARD

Throughout the at standard developmental stage, a strong issue resounds: accountability. Experimental research provides the tools to develop a clear understanding of effect that successfully bridges the gap between wondering and knowing. Findings from carefully crafted experimental studies, presented in the form of reports to all constituents and the general public, lead to a second issue related to this developmental level: policy decisions. Armed with the findings from any of these three studies, policy makers in schools and universities guided toward resolution regarding program adjustments, create new programs or adjust programs to improve instruction and increase learning.

In the first sample study, teachers' implementation of action research projects influenced their understanding of candidates' action research projects. Teachers in the experimental group could account for the importance of conducting action research, due to the lived experience of conducting the same type of research themselves. However, teachers in the control group could not account the reason to conduct the university-required project of conducting action research. The policy instituted by the university, to require an action research project, did not change because of the study but earned the respect of teachers, who in turn, shifted their policy of support for the candidates.

Often in education, successful programs in one setting rarely transfer to other settings unless support for implementation is available. In the second sample study, the results from the Solomon four-group design study of the functional program, developed in one school and transferred to another, suggest program transferability with extended support. The doctoral student/mentor teacher accounted for the veracity of the discourse-writing program. Other schools in the PDS, in search of writing programs that produce results, could use the findings to change policies toward the implementation of the discourse-writing method.

Accounting for expenditures against gains, represented in the last study, potentially influences policy in both universities and schools. The longitudinal study accounted for differences in program effects on three important exit outcomes: retention, achievement, and attitude. The pressure to produce high test scores, for multiple populations in a high stakes testing environment such as the one created by the No Child Left Behind legislation, can sway districts toward teaching that succumbs to the pressure. This study demonstrated that no matter the teacher preparation, test score production remained the same. However, due to the differences in retention and attitude, policies in program support for teacher preparation that produces steady, satisfied teachers.

Accountability and policy development, key in the operation of the at standard developmental stage, become possible through experimental research. The three research samples presented in this chapter hypothetically occurred in a PDS that embraces trust, accountability, and change as a means to academic success. The experimental research design accounts for external and internal validity, rendering the findings generalizable. The generalizability of the findings supports policy changes and further research. The at standard developmental stage, the level of trust among constituents, lends to all forms of research. However, when other forms are employed, the focus on accountability and policy influence remain paramount.

REFERENCES

Hall, Gene, and Shirley Hord. *Implementing Change: Patterns, Principles, and Potholes*. Boston, Mass: Allyn and Bacon, 2001.

Key, James P. "Research Design in Occupational Education." Stillwater, OK: Oklahoma State University, 1997.

Chapter Nine

PDS Research at the Leading Stage

The leading PDS program embodies its title; it leads. Throughout the language of the standard, emphasis on engaging and informing entities outside the original PDS program for the purposes of leading policy changes at local, state, and national levels guides the leading PDS program. The leading PDS program, a long-term functioning entity, provides direction and leadership for PDS programs in the earlier stages of development, going beyond the day to function of a school/university-based partnership. Beginning, developing, and at standard PDS programs seek tools, techniques, information, structure, and assistance from leading PDS programs.

To provide these for other PDS programs, research in the leading PDS transforms to a meta-research level. Leading PDS programs provide conference forums for shared research, discussion of research, think tanks regarding research at varying levels of PDS development, and meta-analyses of published research. The leading PDS takes on an institute/conference form from which other PDS programs draw. In addition, the leading PDS works toward legislative change that systematically supports PDS programs on many levels. Research findings gathered and created by the leading PDS supply the necessary documentation and basis for lobbying legislative decision makers with the intent of changing local, state, and national policies.

SUMMARY OF IMPORTANT LINGUISTIC CHARACTERISTICS

Across the twenty-two elements of the leading stage description, two issues persist: the extension of partnership support and policy change. Examples from the NCATE PDS Standards document regarding the extension of partnership support and policy change, as applied to inquiry, in Standard I include:

- Institutions and local and state entities use PDS generated knowledge to inform policies.
- Multiple avenues for interaction with the profession, family members and policymakers lead to policies and practices that reflect outcomes of PDS work.
- The PDS participants share their inquiry-based learning experiences and results with audiences beyond the local PDS partnership.
- Mechanisms are in place for PDS partners to share results and new knowledge with others in the extended learning community. All learners use their new knowledge to inform practice.
- The PDS participants share their inquiry-based learning experiences and results with audiences beyond the local PDS partnership.

A summary of these statements suggests a PDS program that uses inquiry not only to inform, but bring about change. The extended partnership members generate applicable research and use the results to foster and encourage change beyond the initial PDS program.

Standards II and IV provide additional support for the position of extended partnerships and policy change and include these statements regarding inquiry:

- The PDS partner institutions use the outcomes of continuous assessment, reflection, and actions as the lever for influencing public practices and policies. (II)
- PDS partners present data to the professional and policymaking community showing ways in which they have decreased the gaps in achievement among racial groups. (IV)

The two statements reflect a use of performance data to signify effective programs. The implication that a leading PDS program amasses assessment data to inform outside publics renders this stage of PDS program accountable to both outside sources and other PDS programs.

Throughout all five standards at the leading stage, commentary runs deep regarding policy change. However, only the standards mentioned previously relate directly to inquiry. Policy change occurs at the behest of policymakers, who in the climate of high stakes testing and scientific methods, demand data-driven justification for policy change and support. Consequently, responsibility falls to leading PDS programs to garner the support and change required to sustain PDS programs. This onus born by few PDS programs manifests itself in organizations and institutes, rather than single PDS program's affiliates of universities and schools.

TEAM DEVELOPMENT—TRANSFORMATIONAL

Leading PDS program teams, fully formed and intentional, stand poised to transform PDS programs for others. This developmental stage of PDS examines both internal structures and develops newly formed structures for other developing PDS programs. Accomplished through meta-analysis of research and assessment data, the leading PDS team transforms itself to reach out to policy makers while offering new perspectives on PDS programs to other developing PDS programs. To accomplish this, the team of leading PDS program collaborators work closely with multiple constituents, so that the message remains clear: support PDS through adoptive measures that assure its continuance.

DIMENSIONS OF RESEARCH

The dimensions of research change significantly for the leading PDS program. *Research problems* in the leading PDS program address state and national problems faced by PDS programs. The *research settings* encompass state and national programs. *Research investigators* include researchers across states and national groups who convene to share research that is then analyzed, compiled, reported, and used to influence state and national policy makers. Finally, *research purposes* at the leading level focus on change in policy, attitude, and support. These dimensions suggest a PDS program embroiled in the process of representing rather than initiating.

MATCHED METHODS OF AERA RESEARCH AND NCATE LEADING STAGE

Three of the eight recommended research methods recommended by AERA: historical, case study, and philosophical, seem most appropriate for case making with legislatures. Historical research, rife with experimental and quasi-experimental study results over time, provide the leading PDS with tools to cajole and convince. Case studies of multiple state, regional, and local PDS programs provide leading PDS programs with multiple examples of effects of PDS on learning. Philosophical research, imbued with interpretations and analysis of multiple studies, all of which lead to the same conclusion, provides a tool for leading PDS program researchers to reach out to those unaware of the power and importance of PDS.

Rather than outline three hypothetical research agendas, representing the three recommended here, this part of the chapter documents two leading PDS programs, both generated from universities that eventually became an institute and an organization. The first, the Towson University PDS Network, an institute grew out of a state mandate that all teacher preparation programs train pre-service teachers in PDS programs. Towson conducted its own research for years, but through its contacts with the NCATE Standards developers and through the development of the Maryland PDS Standards, evolved as a leading PDS program. What follows describes the research protocols followed that led to the formation of the institute.

Towson University PDS Network—Leading Stage

Towson University established its first PDS in 1994 with Owings Mills Elementary School in Baltimore County, the 23rd largest school district in the United States. The district surrounds the City of Baltimore (which is a separate school district), is densely populated, and faces many of the same challenges confronted by urban school districts. Changes in the community over time had caused Owings Mills to become a "school in trouble," characterized by low performance on a new state performance assessment, low attendance rates, increased suspensions, and low teacher morale. The principal, who at the time was in the M. Ed. Program at Towson University, had learned about the concept of PDS and made a proposal to the Dean of the College of Education and the Superintendent of Baltimore County Public Schools (BCPS) to create the first PDS in the district. It was the principal's vision to reinvent the school from within, and such a reinvention would require the best teachers possible. The idea of highly qualified master teachers working with teacher candidates in reflective practice provided an attractive new identity for the school and staff. The principal obtained permission from the district to "renew" the school's faculty by requiring all the teachers to reapply for their positions following a formal presentation from the university about the concept of PDS and what the partnership could do for the school. Teachers who chose to stay as well as new hires underwent a series of interviews in a collaborative process between the district and the university. Finally, a new "boundary spanner" position was created in which two full-time instructional facilitators were paid jointly by the university and the district to coordinate teacher preparation and professional development in the newly formed PDS.

The Owings Mills PDS program involved a cohort of 16 undergraduate teacher candidates in elementary education who self-selected to participate in this alternative placement rather than regular student teaching. The cohort spent its entire teacher preparation program (junior and senior years) at the school, having all course work delivered on site in a classroom dedicated for the use of the PDS. The program was rich with integrated experiences for the candidates and mentor teachers, including bus tours of the school's neighborhood, field trips focusing on diversity issues, such as the National Holocaust Museum in Washington, D. C., conferences and retreats featuring nationally known experts on curriculum and school improvement, and graduate courses offered at a reduced rate and delivered at the school. Mentor teachers also participated in a yearlong professional development seminar in which they developed a performance assessment/observation tool for providing feedback to teacher candidates. Mentor teachers and teacher candidates also participated in workshops where they learned how to create performance assessments that would help students become successful on the state's testing program. Partnership activities at the time were funded by the Eisenhower Professional State Grant Program and the Goals 2000 Grant Program.

In 1995, the state issued a policy mandate that requires all teacher candidates in state approved teacher preparation programs to undergo a yearlong internship (two consecutive semesters) in a professional development school. Because Towson University is the largest provider of new teachers to the state, scaling up its PDS was imperative. By 2001, virtually all of its teacher candidates—both undergraduate and MAT in early childhood, elementary, secondary, and special education—were placed in PDS partnerships. By 2007, the university's PDS network had grown to more than 70 clusters (multiple sites working together as single partnerships) in nine school districts in the metropolitan area.

As PDS activity began to develop in the state and the nation, the accomplishments of the Owings Mills-Towson University PDS became known through presentations at national conferences, such as the American Association of Colleges for Teacher Education (AACTE). In 1998, the partnership gained national recognition as a Distinguished Program in Teacher Education by the Association of Teacher Educators (ATE). The partnership gained further distinction in 1999-2001 when it served as one of the pilot sites that field-tested the NCATE PDS Standards in which it completed a self-study and underwent a site visit by a panel of national PDS experts. The most important commendation given by NCATE was "the partnership has served as a lever for change in the educational reform movement at both the school and university level and as a model for PDS development in the larger professional community locally, regionally, and nationally" (p. 18). The partnership was also commended for its serious and sustained attention to learning by all its members and its strong commitment to meeting the learning needs of all students. It was recommended that the partnership should "consider developing a partnership-wide vision of what a *collegial* program of inquiry and action research should involve as well as how participants could use their skills to implement such a program. This might involve thinking of inquiry as group deliberation on problems of practice focused on achievement test scores and teaching strategies, examination of student work, or the improvement of mentoring strategies for interns" (p. 18). Also, it was recommended that the partnership put in place an infrastructure to ensure better communication and dialogue for all stakeholder groups. Finally, it was recommended that the partnership should "find ways to highlight and celebrate its diversity in the PDS and its community" (p. 19).

In response to the recommendations to further develop inquiry and action research, the Dean of the College of Education proposed establishing a PDS research institute in 2001. The institute was comprised of university faculty and administrators from the College of Education, the College of Liberal Arts, and the College of Science and Mathematics; teachers and administrators from the partnering school districts; and a representative from NCATE. A faculty member who had coordinated the NCATE project was appointed chair of the institute. The institute's purpose was to preserve the history of the Towson PDS, educate the wider community about the issues of PDS work, and conduct improvement-oriented inquiry.

The state Department of Education awarded $30,000 to help launch the institute. The first project undertaken was the publication of a series of contributed books. The first book told the Towson story in which university faculty and administrators, mentor teachers, principals and district administrators, and former candidates collaboratively authored chapters that described the details of how the network had been established. The book served as a vehicle not only for disseminating the Towson story but also for bringing together the constituents in a focused activity for reflection and renewal of the network. The second book contained research presented at a national PDS conference hosted by the university in 2003. Contributors represented twelve partnerships in nine states, and topics ranged from establishing PDS in music education and physical education to assessing PDS by using the standards. For the third book, contributors were drawn from PDS researchers who were active in national networks, such as AERA, AACTE, and the newly formed National Association for Professional Development Schools (NAPDS). In their chapters, the authors examined critical issues in PDS, such as research and evaluation, processes and outcomes, leadership, and diversity, equity, and social justice.

In addition to supporting the book series, the state funding supported a longitudinal study of the retention of eighty-seven Towson graduates hired as new teachers by BCPS in 2000. The class of 2000 presented an opportunity for making comparisons between PDS- and non-PDS prepared candidates because, at that point in time, approximately half the candidates were in PDS placements and half were in traditional student teaching. (After 2000, virtually all candidates were in PDS placements per the state's mandate.) Findings from the study showed that after five years, 70 percent of the PDS prepared teachers were still teaching in the district compared with 34 percent of the non-PDS prepared teachers ($p < .05$). Findings from interviews also showed that PDS prepared teachers revealed a strong focus on (1) reflection and thoughtfulness in planning and assessment; (2) consideration for what is developmentally appropriate for students, especially regarding the diverse composition of one's classroom; and (3) considerations for the physical and psychological environment in which teaching and learning occur, e.g., how time, space, materials, groups, and social interactions support learning. Follow-up interviews with the same teachers in 2006 showed connections to their PDS preparation. Teachers felt that learning to teach in a PDS had accelerated their performance, making them more realistic and confident in their teaching. They also felt more prepared to take on leadership roles in their schools as a result of understanding how the *whole* school operated, not just their classroom. Strong relationships with cooperating teachers and university faculty and supervisors provided support that often continued into their professional teaching. Participation in outreach activities such as service learning and action research projects, compelled them to become more involved with the school, thus making them educational "insiders" from the start of their careers.

This study, which was predicated on trust and a good working relationship between the university and district, was brought to the attention of the state superintendent of schools, the state higher education commission, the state school board, the governor, and the state legislature through a series of meetings in which the Dean and Associate Dean of the College of Education gave testimony. This study, combined with the examination of other data, such as the cost to universities for operating PDS, the cost to school districts as a result of teacher attrition, and, ultimately, the impacts on student achievement, was the catalyst for the appropriation of approximately 2 million dollars in the state's budget for professional development schools. Conditions for receiving the funds were that each partnership would (1) conduct its own teacher retention study, thus tracking its graduates for several years, and (2) implement a systematic study of how PDS activity impacted student achievement in its partnership.

In response to this accomplishment and its attendant accountability, the Dean of the College of Education called for a reexamination of the institute's mission and vision. Rather than remaining a small-scale venture, the institute would establish a data base that could be used for large scale studies of PDS within the Towson network, across the state, and beyond. Warehousing large data sets, including data about the context of PDS, would enable all constituents to have access to information for conducting carefully designed comparative studies, either as individuals or as collaborators with other PDS partners and PDS networks. Thus, the institute would become a vehicle for effecting change in policy and best practices of PDS in the state and the nation.

The second leading PDS program, initiated from the University of South Carolina after many years of program building and influencing policy locally and in the state of South Carolina, formed an association as an outreach to other PDS programs conducting research on PDS. What follows, a direct excerpt from the NAPDS website (www.napds.org), describes the protocols followed that led to the formation of the organization. The call is for dialogue, research on PDS and drive for policy change that supports PDS programs.

A Brief History of the National Association for Professional Development Schools

The University of South Carolina began co-sponsoring a PDS National Conference in March 2000. That initial event, held in Columbia, South Carolina, attracted approximately six hundred educators and was such a success that the university continued sponsoring similar conferences on an annual basis for the next five years.

In 2002 the conference moved from South Carolina to Orlando, Florida, and by 2005 had begun to attract close to one thousand PDS educators from nearly every state in the nation. Individuals who attended the conferences repeatedly expressed appreciation for the hands-on and practical nature of the conference presentations and pointed out time and again two aspects which they believed were unique to the event: (1) a near-equal balance of university and preK-12 educators and (2) an exclusive focus on issues relevant to Professional Development Schools. Nowhere else, participants noted, had they found the opportunity to share ideas with such a wide breadth of P-20 educators and been able to focus solely on PDS concerns unencumbered by other admittedly important, yet non-PDS specific, educational issues.

The desire to discuss PDS-specific concerns with other educators who shared an interest in and passion for PDS work led to a conversation at the 2003 National Conference about the feasibility of creating a professional association which would encourage year-round PDS dialogue. The seventy-five individuals who participated in that conversation immediately agreed that such an association was much needed, and so a handful of volunteers met in Columbia, South Carolina, in November 2003, to begin the process of making the association a reality. They shared their initial efforts with participants at the March 2004 National Conference and encouraged others to join them in the planning process. That call produced a Founding Organizational Committee, eventually consisting of eighteen educators from eleven states, which met throughout the next year to revise a mission statement drafted at the first meeting and to design both a constitutional structure and a list of goals for the association. As they did so, they kept in mind that the primary goal was to create a professional association that, in the words of one of the group members, would enhance the capacity of PDS educators to do their work. With that overall goal in mind, the group agreed to: (1) establish a leadership structure which would represent a balance across the educational continuum; (2) develop a website to allow members access to resources and a venue for on-going dialogue; (3) circulate a newsletter to disseminate best practices, pertinent news, and PDS-related announcements; (4) produce a periodic journal to circulate evaluative research, successful programmatic models, and naturalistic inquiry in the PDS community; and (5) join with the University of South Carolina in sponsoring the annual PDS National Conference and, in doing so, continue the commitment to balanced participation and focused presentations.

By the time of the March 2005 PDS National Conference, the association planners had appointed an Interim Executive Council which worked throughout 2004 and early 2005 to put into place the nuts and bolts of a working association. That group obtained start-up funds from individual and institutional founders and benefactors and, through the respective generosity of Towson University and the University of Missouri, began work on the inaugural newsletter and the creation of an association website. The Council decided that the initial membership of the association would be comprised of those individuals who attended the 2005 Conference, and so it drafted Association By-Laws which were subsequently approved by that membership at an NAPDS Celebration on the afternoon of Friday, March 18, 2005. The membership at that time also approved the removal of the "interim" label from the Executive Council, approved a Fall 2005 election process for new officers to be installed at the 2006 National Conference, and in taking these actions officially launched an association which had been two years in the making.

What these two leading PDS programs have in common—a drive to change local, state, and national policy through research—demonstrates the difference between this level and all others. While both leading PDS programs began as university/school based initiatives, both grew beyond the concerns for local internal needs to larger ones that reached out to all developmental levels of PDS programs. To reach the leading stage requires vision, perseverance, tenacity, and a tightly woven team of collaborators, all aiming for the same goal: policy change and recognition of PDS as a viable program of teacher preparation.

REFERENCE

"Standards for Professional Development Schools." Washington, D.C.: National Council for Accreditation of Teacher Education, 2001.

Chapter Ten

Summary

Throughout this book, the authors have established a rationale for creating a framework that provides a developmental approach for research on professional development schools. The framework was created in order to assist researchers and practitioners in their decision making for designing and implementing research that is appropriate to partnerships' developmental stages yet of such a quality as to effect change for schools, teachers, and children. The premise of the book is based on an alignment of operational language found in the NCATE PDS Standards and AERA recommended research methods and reflects the collaborative as well as personal opinions and interpretations of the authors based on their experience as PDS researchers and practitioners.

Professional development schools are at a crossroads in the current environment of standards and accountability along the entire PreK-16 continuum of schooling. Many PDSs are entering their second decade of existence while others have faded away and new ones are beginning. When revisiting the visions for PDS presented by The Holmes Group and NCATE, one wonders if those goals can be attained let alone sustained into the next generation of PDS work. Undoubtedly, there has been a preponderance of writing about PDS. The publications analyzed in this book, not to mention the many presentations given at numerous PDS and teacher education-related conferences in the United States, Canada, and Europe, attest to an immeasurable amount of time and talent spent on trying to discern the complexity of PDS and its effects.

Yet, the authors, as well as others, have found and criticized the fact that the overabundance of process research, single-site case studies, and studies that do not demonstrate causality do not carry the *influence* needed to effect substantive and widespread change in policies and best practices for PDS as a model of school reform. The paucity of research on issues pertaining to diversity, equity, and social justice—a major focus of the PDS agenda—is also a concern. In order to attain this vision, more collaboration for ways and means for PDS research—including the creation of tools, frameworks, and schema to assist in research design—is needed to get the job done.

One of the most satisfying aspects of being engaged in PDS work is the multiple opportunities to collaborate with many diverse, knowledgeable, and talented colleagues at the state, regional, national, and even international, levels. Within the past few years dialogues and exchanges about the condition of PDS research have begun within and between members and leaders of the various professional organizations, including the PDS Research Special Interest Group (SIG) of AERA, the National Association for Professional Development Schools (NAPDS), The Holmes Partnership, the National Network for Educational Renewal (NNER), the American Association of Colleges for Teacher Education (AACTE), the Association of Teacher Educators (ATE), as well as their many state and regional affiliates, and other state and regional PDS networks, collaboratives, and consortia.

A newcomer to the PDS-related professional groups is the National Consortium of Professional Development Schools (NCPDS). NCPDS is a collaborative project that currently involves 40 institutions of higher education in partnership with more than 300 PDSs in all regions of the United States. NCPDS was established in 2004 with a grant from the United States Department of Education's Fund for the Improvement of Post Secondary Education (FIPSE) and provides a comprehensive, easily accessible, and practice-informed resource through which institutions can contribute to and learn from each other's experiences within the highly contextualized and complex work of PDS.

The project uses Microsoft® Office SharePoint Portal Server 2003 to create a collaborative web-based environment as a resource for the continuous improvement of educator preparation and P-12 practice in the service of improved student learning and achievement. A national Advisory Board guides NCPDS development, and a team of technology experts at Georgia Southwestern State University manages and maintains the site.

The key feature of the web-based environment—and of special interest to those looking for a tool to help PDS partnerships self-assess their stage of development—is the *PDS Impact Profile*. The *PDS Impact Profile* is aligned with the NCATE PDS Standards (2001) and is an adaptation of the Maryland State Department of Education Developmental Guidelines for Maryland Professional Development Schools (2003). This interactive tool allows users to click on their "standing" according to the indicators for Learning Community; Collaboration; Accountability; Organization, Roles, and Resources; and Diversity and Equity. Text boxes allow users to add links to their artifacts, thus creating a repository of evidence for using the standards, and a *Summary Report* allows members to see their partnership's levels of development at a glance. Readers who would like to learn more about NCPDS should visit http://pds.gsw.edu/ and click on General Information to preview the website.

Thus, like the highly interrelational institution that it is, the PDS continues to transform itself by being ever-responsive to the learning needs of all its members and embracing new ideas and new approaches. All constituents must take the time to think seriously about the issues facing PDS as a center for improvement-oriented inquiry and working collaboratively to take the steps necessary for finding those solutions. Through such actions, the PDS movement will be better situated to continue to grow as a major force for improving the quality of teaching and learning for everybody's children.

Appendix

12 STEP PLAN
APPLYING THE FRAMEWORK
PDS PROGRAM RESEARCH

Step 1: As a team, make the decision to conduct research on the PDS program.

Step 2: As a team, decide on the research expertise in the group of PDS workers.

Step 3: Go to http://www.ncate.org/public/pdsSelfStudy.asp?ch=139, and get a copy of the NCATE PDS self study guide.

Step 4: As a team, conduct the self study and determine the Developmental Level of your PDS.

Step 5: Go to either Chapter 6,7,8, or 9 in this book, and determine which research methods best suit your developmental level.

Step 6: As a team, determine a problem to study in the PDS program.

Step 7: As a team, pose a research question.

Step 8: As a team, pose a hypothesis for the outcome of the research of the question.

Step 9: As a team, decide on the most appropriate method(s) for your research project.

Step 10: Conduct the research and collect data.

Step 11: Analyze the data.

Step 12: Present results in a report, public presentation at a conference, and/or publication.

Index

Adequate Yearly Progress (AYP), expectations and, 25

AERA Research Methods: beginning stage of, 36–37; case study research and, 33; comparative experimental research and, 34; developing stage and, 37–38; ethnographic research and, 33; framework for developmental approach and, 35–36; framework using and, 31–40; historical research and, 32; leading stage and, 39; matched methods of, 44–52; philosophic research and, 32; quasi-experimental research and, 34–35; standard stage and, 38–39; summary and, 97–99; survey research and, 33–34

American Association of Colleges of Teacher Education (AACTE), PDS programs and, 91

American Educational Research Association (AERA), accepted practices in teacher preparation and, 1

ANCOVA: analyzing data and, 81–84; testing and, 77

articles: Accountability Era: 2001–2006, 27–28; Beginning Era: 1988–1990, 26; Functioning Era: 1995–2000, 27; Growing Era: 1991–1994, 26

Arts-Based programs: data review and, 66; Mayan culture and, 65–66

Arts-Based Research, overview of, 31–32, 69

Association of Teacher Educators (ATE), PDS programs and, 91

Beginning Stage: Standard I: Learning Community, 42; Standard II: Accountability, 42; Standard IV: Diversity and Equity, 42

Bell, Terrell, *The Nation at Risk* report, 21

"boundary spanner" position, teacher preparation and, 90

Bruner, Jerome, *The Process of Education* and, 19

"career", idea of, 7

Case Study: action research project and, 62; AERA Research Methods and, 44–47; Sample Historical Study, 50–52; Sample Survey Study, 47–49

collaboration, standards for, 15–16

comparative experimental research, overview of, 34